Mixed-Media NATURE JOURNALS

Mixed-Media NATURE JOURNALS

New Techniques for Exploring Nature, Life, and Memory

L.K. LUDWIG

QUARRY BOOKS

BEVERLY MASSACHUSETTS

First published in the United States of America by
Quarry Books, a member of
Quayside Publishing Group
100 Cummings Center
Suite 406-L
Beverly, Massachusetts 01915-6101
Telephone: (978) 282-9590
Fax: (978) 283-2742
www.quarrybooks.com

Library of Congress Cataloging-in-Publication Data
Ludwig, L. K.
Mixed-media nature journals : new techniques for exploring nature, life, and memories / L.K. Ludwig.
p. cm.
ISBN 1-59253-367-1
1. Photograph albums. 2. Scrapbooks. I. Title.
TR501.L84 2006
745.593--dc22

2007019573
CIP

ISBN-13: 978-1-59253-367-1
ISBN-10: 1-59253-367-1

10 9 8 7 6 5 4 3 2 1

Design: Laura H. Couallier, Laura Herrmann Design
Photography: Al Mallette, Lightstream

Printed in Singapore

A dream tree, Polly's tree:
a thicket of sticks,
T
21

"Let the beauty
of what you love,
be what you do."

—Rumi

The Woodland Fern Journal features mesh printing, page 54, and dry and salt printing, page 45.

Contents

Rather than being arranged chronologically, entries in this vintage account ledger turned nature journal, are arranged alphabetically using the existing divider tabs.

Introduction

Nature calls to our very spirits, asking us to notice. We stoop to gather small, smooth pebbles for our pockets, tiny flowers wink at us from the grass, and fistfuls of blazing, colored leaves make their way into our hands. With nature, we stay childlike in our awe, and our sense of magic and mystery is nurtured. We point at sunsets and gaze at the moon. The sticks and feathers that make their way into our pockets and onto our windowsills and dusty shelves bear witness to our desire to record those moments when we have been touched by nature.

For many of us, we long to chronicle our experience of nature, yet we feel that our drawing or painting skills are insufficient to do so. We are drawn to books on nature journaling, and we gather blank books and tiny watercolor sets, like magpies gathering shiny silver bits. We gaze upon our supplies with longing, perhaps taking them out now and then, only to be sorely disappointed with our results. We resolve someday, someday, to take a class.

There is a solution to this desire, one that rings honest and true in our hearts, one that is readily available, and one that will allow us to work with what we see, what we hear, and what we feel on those morning walks and evening saunters. The answer: using a variety of traditional techniques in nontraditional ways. This allows us to enter the magpie-like world of the mixed-media arts.

"Nature will bear the closest inspection. She invites us to lay our eye level with her smallest leaf, and take an insect view of the plain."

—Henry David Thoreau

"I believe there is a subtle magnetism in Nature, which if we unconsciously yield to it, will direct us aright."

– Henry David Thoreau

An accordion-fold-style journal with the pages enclosed in mica, page 86

Content and Meaning

chapter 1

One of my fondest memories is of the time when I realized I was a 'maker' of things. I was eight years old, riding in the back of the family station wagon. These were pre-seatbelt, pre-booster seat days, so I was lying on a nest of blankets, book resting on my chest, watching the landscape and the sky go by the car window. We were headed to the shore, and I was taking snapshots. Not snapshots with a camera, but with my eyes: I would capture the image by screwing my eyes tightly closed to contain what beauty I saw, and commit the image to memory so I could later recall that exact moment. Clouds, forests and fallen trees, rusty bridges, and forgotten creeks were gathered this way during the long fifteen-hour drive. On that day, my secret longing to record this beauty was born; I became an artist.

It wasn't until decades later, however, before I could begin to identify myself to other people as an artist. When I was in my early thirties, my father passed away, and with some of the small amount of money I inherited, I purchased a good tent and a medium format camera. I also fell in love, moved to western Pennsylvania, and began work at another university. One day I plucked up the courage and headed over to the art department to inquire about post-baccalaureate admission. No one laughed, and my artistic journey began. Yes, I was still tromping about the woods, but this time my camera was in my hand. Many aspiring writers are told to "write what you know." This is my approach to art. I work with what I know—the fields I drive by on my morning commute, the river and mountains at our river house, the woods behind my house where I sometimes walk, the creek at my in-law's house, the trees, the water, the stones and leaves that decorate the landscape. I weave the threads of nature together with the threads of my life to create work that is both autobiographical and nature-oriented.

Journal keeping is certainly "writing what you know," but I would change that phrase to "making art about what you know." By that, I mean turning the artistic techniques in your repertoire, and those you acquire from books, magazines, and workshops, to what you see in nature that touches you. You needn't live in wide, open spaces or in the deep woods to do this. Daily walks in a neighborhood park, weekend drives to the country, or the fields on the side of the roads you drive by en route to work are all there for visual mining. Vacations, the changing seasons, your favorite picnic spot; these are all rich and wonderful topics to explore in your nature journal. You don't need to be able to draw—you only need to be able to see.

Toward Meaningful, Personal Work

Even as artists, we pick up messages from our consumer-driven society: buy these products and supplies, master this technique, use this sort of embellishment. As artists we are naturally intrigued, so we acquire supplies and tools that sometimes go unused after the first try. We are carried along by the enthusiasm of articles in magazines, and we try the techniques and products they portray. There is nothing at all wrong with this. Trying new products and techniques on for size is how we expand our visual language. If you think of every technique as a vocabulary word, and artwork that makes use of various techniques as sentences, each skill or technique you master adds depth to your visual vocabulary, expanding your mastery of your own visual language.

Much has been said, of late, about copying the work one sees in magazines or workshops. There is a significant difference between copying to learn, which has been an honored teaching and learning technique since the art academies of the Renaissance, and copying as thievery. When you learn a technique and begin practicing it over and over, at first the style of the work produced is reminiscent of the teacher, but practicing embeds the skills in our hands. Over time. the new skills mingle with our other skills and the work becomes uniquely our own. Don't be afraid of trying on a technique for size. Does it resonate with you, or do you feel as though you are forcing it? What draws you to the technique? Is it the colors of the paint? Examine the color palette used and think about why those colors appeal to you. Where do they connect in your life? Is it because the artwork looks aged or care worn? What does that say to you; is it about time and memory? Explore why you are attracted to a technique, a style, or a color palette, and over time you will integrate those things in an honest way in your own style, in your own work. This is part of the process of growing as an artist.

If you collect a particular type of object, consider why you are drawn to that object. Make a list of the symbolism associated with that type of object, what it represents in the world at large, what it represents to you. Armed with this information, think about what you are communicating when you use that object in your work. I collect feathers, so I learned that they often symbolize birds, angels, flight, freedom, or the loss of freedom (through the loss of the feathers). As I examine what feathers mean to me, I realize that I am drawn to birds; their ability to fly seems magical to me. For me, birds are connected to beauty and mystery. By using feathers in my work I can represent or express that awe, or the magic of flight, or the way that I seem to have anthropomorphized birds. In addition to using feathers, I can include other objects based on my thoughts and feelings. I am drawn to bird's nests for the way they echo home and bird's eggs for the way that they represent children—both topics very dear to my daily existence.

As I work on a topic, I continue to ask questions. When I work with spring as a season am I thinking of spring and renewal? When I work with wintertime, am I thinking about loss? These two very separate thought paths generate completely different feelings, images, and colors. By examining why we gather and collect what we do, we can gain insight into our artistic symbolism and incorporate our symbols in a purposeful way in our work.

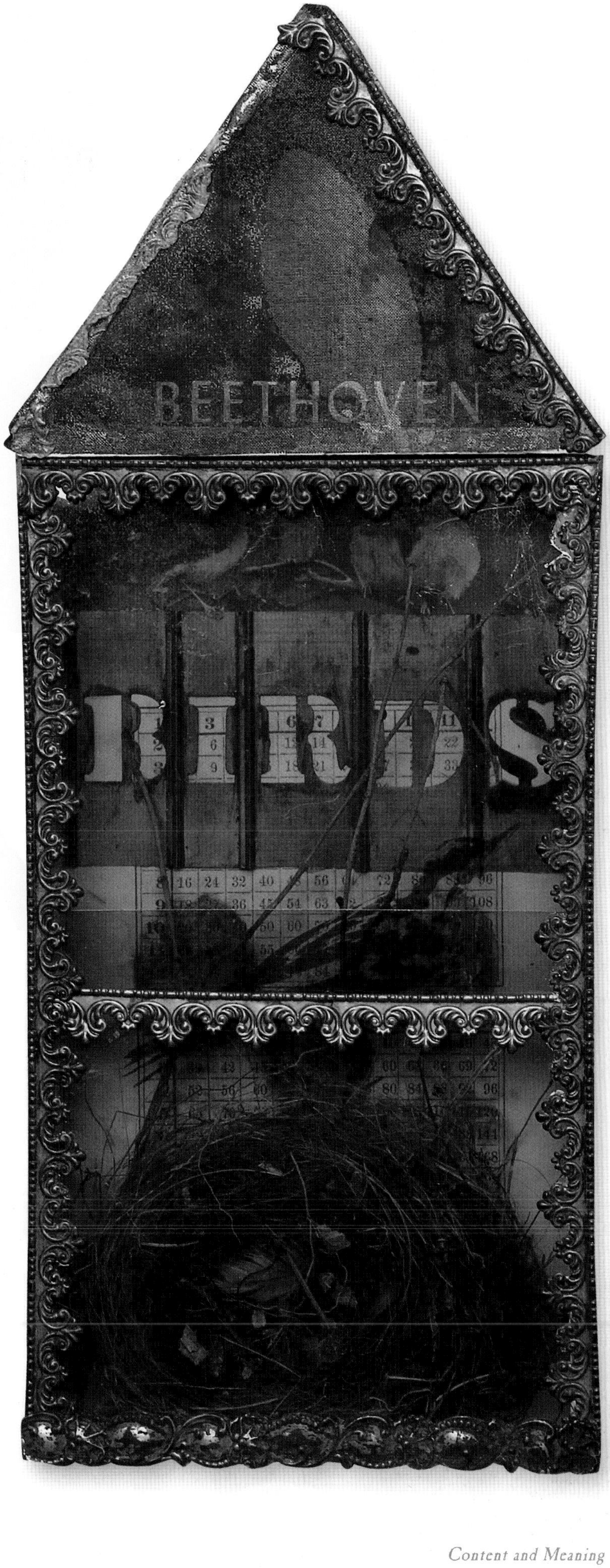

This cover piece is from a journal that focuses on bird-related images as a way to explore family relationships.

October Journal, showing author's way of using nature journaling to express feelings as described in the text on the following page.

> *"The invariable mark of wisdom is to see the miraculous in the common."*
>
> —Ralph Waldo Emerson

When nature journaling, the most meaningful page content is connected to our daily lives, our personal current events. What is going on for us, and what is on our minds, is carried into our relationship with the natural world. Our ponderings while we walk through the park, what is pressing on our minds as we watch the geese rise off the pond, our joys and worries as we drive along sunlit fields of corn, impact our relationship to these sights. When working from a personal, meaningful place, we acknowledge this process and mine it for artistic content.

Ask yourself a few key questions when mining for personal content:

- What was on my mind?
- What feelings led me to choose this content?
- What feelings am I trying to communicate?
- What colors are associated with these feelings? What colors are in my imagery? Is there overlap? How can I connect these color palettes?
- Are there techniques I can use to support communication of my content?
- Consider shiny transparencies and colorful collage for hopefulness, a patina of metal and rusty earthy colors for the passage of time, or scrubbed painted surfaces built in layers for nostalgia.

I often drive along black asphalt country roads, bordered by sunlit fall cornstalks, and I roll down the window of my car, hearing the sound of the dried stalks rustling in the wind, and smelling the scent of autumn leaves in the breeze. I am thinking about my day job, my family, and the time crunch. Suddenly, as the late afternoon light brightens the fields, they seem to take on a surreal, nostalgic postcard quality. I feel my heart squeeze as I miss my children terribly in that very minute. I stop the car and shoot some photographs. Later, when I use those photographs in a journal, I have stained the pages with coffee to age them into that nostalgic place, and I use Polaroid transfers to communicate the surreal feeling I felt that day. I incorporate images of my children in the autumn to connect my feelings for them, or my longings, into my artwork. I use interleaving paper to replicate that sound of the rustling stalks. In this way, I have expressed my experience of that moment near the fields with honest, personal meaning, without extensive writing, but with my unique artistic vision.

Gather up materials that both look and feel related to the topic you are working on and toss them into a small box or basket. For me, these could include scraps of paper in colors related to my palette, images from my collection of antique and vintage natural history books, photographs, outcasts from other projects, sticks, stones, shells, feathers, bones, teeth, or bits of text. As you work on a journal, edit your pile, adding and subtracting. Consider going out to collect leaves or flowers with which to make prints on paper or metal mesh. Begin to manipulate particular images using a computer, copier, or mark-making materials. This gives a way to begin the work.

Whether your topic is specific to a location, or a season, whether you are exploring a theme in your work, or creating a rich source of visual information to draw from for designs for other art media, the critical takeaway is to work from your own thoughts, feelings, and experiences.

Creating a Location-Based Journal

Certain places and geographic locations inspire us. Whether we have visited that place only once, on rare occasions, or regularly, we all have outdoor locations in our history that have given us meaningful experiences. Vacations, a regular path we walk in the evenings, a weekend home, the roads we drive on our daily commute, our own yard or land, have given us gifts that we can in turn express in a journal.

These places, these outdoor spaces where nature has touched us, are in a way sacred. By sacred, I am not necessarily referring to a religious connection, although many people throughout history have been moved in that direction by the wonder of nature. What I mean by sacred is the sense of awe or wonder at things large and small; the incredible beauty of a small purple wildflower, the soaring majesty of an eagle, or the immense power of the ocean's waves on the shore.

Photographs give us entry into the process of creating a location-based journal. Whether an ongoing series, or one set from a special trip, the images we have taken provide a backbone for reminding us what it is that touches us about a special place.

"How strange that Nature does not knock, and yet does not intrude!"

– Emily Dickinson

A journal box filled with artwork, found objects, and artificial materials related to a specific location.

"World, you are beautifully dressed."

—William Brighty Rands

GENERATING A COLOR PALETTE

Take a minute to think about your location. When you recall your location, are you thinking about morning, afternoon, or evening? Perhaps even night? Is the light cool or warm? Maybe you are watching the morning mist burn off the river with the sunrise. Perhaps it is the full moon, silver and cool, lighting the birches. Or maybe it is both of these things. Make some quick notes about what you have recalled, the light, and what colors come to mind with these places and instances. List at least three colors for each place. If you can find visual references for these colors in paints, photos, or magazine snippets, put them where you can view them. These can give you a starting palette for your pages, a jumping off point from which to work.

OUTSIDE SOURCES FOR IMAGERY

Maps, brochures, and postcards can provide additional images related to a location. In addition, your own personal ephemera—the wine label from the bottle you shared with friends around the fire, a snippet of poetry that takes you to that exact place in your mind—are all useful for creating pages. Consider using an Internet site such as www.ebay.com or a second-hand shop to locate vintage postcards, maps, and books about your location. Don't overlook the actual natural items from your location such as pebbles, leaves, twigs, and flowers. Also, vintage books on flowers, birds, trees, and other flora and fauna can add visual interest to your pages.

YOUR ORIGINAL PHOTOS

How might the visual references you have collected fit in with your photographs? Will the images need the softening impact of ink-jet transfers, or should they be layered over other images as a transparency? Will you sand a photograph to highlight just part of an image, or select an area of the photograph and enlarge it to the size of the page? Will converting an image to black and white or creating a photo negative create the sense of mystery you need?

Image transfer of an original photo; note how the cool-toned palette and the wet appearance of the vegetation communicate detail about the day spent on this particular beach.

OTHER CONSIDERATIONS

If your location is one you visit regularly, you may want to work your journal pages to show the location over time. If your visit to a location was a one-time experience, then create an artist book in honor of that visit.

Are there other people involved in your experience? Perhaps a spouse, partner, children, or friends that are part of your experience? You may wish to include them directly or symbolically, with meaningful journaling about the shared experience.

Are there sounds associated with your location? An owl's hooting? A train whistle? The raucous cawing of crows? What about scents? Pine needles fragrant underfoot, the wet smell of vegetation in the rain, the scent of the sea? While you may not be able to include the actual scent, you can depict the source of your olfactory memory using images or other embellishments.

Creating a Seasons-Based Journal

Winter, spring, summer, and fall; the path the earth travels around the sun. Depending on where you live, the seasons mean different things. I live in the Northeast portion of the United States, so winter holidays mean snowflakes and ice on the surface of little streams, rainy Aprils, parched August days, and gorgeous displays of color on the trees in the fall, at least until the November rains whisk them into sodden piles. Friends in Australia celebrate the Christmas holiday while on summer vacation, and friends in California can pick tangerines from a tree in their yard in February. Wherever you are, whether the changes are subtle or pronounced, nature is a dynamic force and the changes—even subtle—are always evident. Plants have growing cycles; birds nest, fledglings fly and mature into adults, and the cycle begins again.

The possibilities for working with the seasons as an area of exploration feels practically limitless. Here are some ideas:

- Choose one season and chronicle that season in your journal.
- Explore a location through all four seasons or one season over the course of years.
- Use the seasons as a basis for regular journaling, incorporating both nature and daily life.
- Choose a season and a loved one and journal about that time frame, including both the past and the present.
- Compare and contrast seasons on alternating pages.
- Choose a theme and use the seasons as a way to structure your journal.
- Follow a part of nature through the seasons; for example, trees, birds, or flowers.
- Examine the season of your birthday and use images of your self across time; alternatively, use self portraits to explore a visual, autobiographical experience of nature.
- Work around your sense of smell; what is the scent of the seasons? What imagery and color palettes do these scents generate?

Seasons often seem to have a pre-set color palette based depending on your geographic location. This pattern of color that shifts throughout the year is often accompanied by a change in the hue of light; harsher, darker, cooler, warmer. You can reflect the changing qualities of light in your journal with washes of color, your photographs, and even paper color. For example, printmaking papers come in white, cream, and grey hues. This can change the mood of the page without adding any pigment over the work. Working with starker images or black-and-white images during the dormant season can dramatically communicate barren winter sights. Incorporating the immense variety of greens during the verdant fertile burst of late spring can provide a wealth of journal fodder. You needn't be limited by the traditional palette for the season; walking about on a snowy winter day, in addition to the dark of bare branches and white of the snow, you will find the bright red of a cardinal feather, the burgundy of fruit left on ornamental trees, a range of blues and silvers, and the papery thin ochre colors of dried leaf skeletons.

"Let us love winter, for it is the spring of genius."

—Pietro Aretino

The Seasons Journal cover was created by using an old Scrabble board as a painting surface; the spine was constructed by creating a very small patchwork quilt embellished with fibers.

This winter-themed journal uses imagery, poetry, and a color palette that evokes the chosen season.

Often our emotional states are echoed by the seasons. In the Northeast, February's relentless chill and gray skies cause many conversations about the unending winter and boredom or depression: the winter blahs. Spring carries a sense of renewal, of hope or opportunity. Autumn can signal change or abundance. When working with a season, consider both its traditional symbolism and the meaning that season holds for you. For example, while symbolically the current interpretation of fall is harvest and preparation for winter, for me fall represents the new year, and I am somehow more creative at this time than any other. I might then choose a brighter fall palette than if I felt fall was the precursor to the long sleep of a dark winter.

Another way to bring in significant personal content is to work in autobiographical terms around the seasons. With the turning of the seasons, the passage of time, comes history. In keeping with the "make art about what you know" concept, consider working from a historical perspective using your life, your family, or your feelings about a parent, your marriage, and your children to provide a way to work personal content in keeping with the season's natural content. The images needn't be literal, and can include snippets of letters, quotes from poetry and prose that remind you of something, or symbolic references to persons or events from seasons past.

In nature journaling, it is practically impossible to avoid the impact of the seasons on your work. While we might have focused on the minutia of the woods when collecting acorns, twigs, tiny green fiddleheads, and russet leaves, creating around the broader topic of the seasons can remind us to see the forest and the trees. The full landscape, the light, the flora and fauna, even the debris we collect changes, making the seasons a rich area of exploration and discovery for nature journalers.

"Autumn is a second spring when every leaf is a flower."

—Albert Camus

Exploring a Theme

Creating a theme in your journal is one of the easiest ways of framing the content, thereby opening a way to include meaningful ideas related to your life and to your experience of nature.

Specific natural themes that are related to a particular item or type of object such as trees, birds, gardens, rocks, feathers, shells, or flowers, all provide wonderful fodder to create not one journal, but dozens.

Broader themes, such as the concept of dynamic change, the presence of the past in the current moment, or the idea of the land holding history, offer an opportunity to explore larger ideas that might translate to other art works as well.

Another way to work in a nature journal is to choose a favorite bit of writing—poetry, prose, or a collection of quotes—and create a journal around those words. You can journal a page about a selected writing or create an entire journal around one text.

The Oak, by Alfred, Lord Tennyson, provides the inspiration and structural backbone of this journal.

CREATING A DESIGN SOURCEBOOK

If you work in other areas, a mixed-media nature journal provides the perfect opportunity to explore designs based in your experience of the natural world. Whether we realize it or not, we are profoundly influenced by natural shapes; designs either echo natural shapes or are created in opposition to them. You can derive wonderful designs for use in other media from the work in your nature journals.

Archetypes and symbols may begin to appear in your work and in your mixed-media pieces, you may find yourself drawn to specific types of trees, flowing water, birds, deer, or clouds. These symbolic elements may make their way into other paintings and paper works. The exploration of nature's color palette as it relates to your life can lead you to using those color ways in other work.

Shapes begin to echo throughout different pieces. I am drawn to streams and rivers full of rocks that fascinate me with their rounded shapes in varying sizes. The color palettes of these stream beds often include a startling pop of some other color, turned into small sketches of ovals and circles and in layers, and these shapes wend their way into collages, ceramic pieces, and jewelry. The linear repetition within a field of hay or the light and dark of the tall grasses moving in a summer wind can find their way into a block carving to be used for pressing silver clay jewelry.

The Oak Journal

"I believe a leaf of grass is no less than the journey-work of the stars."

—Walt Whitman

"Use the talents you possess—for the woods would be a very silent place if no birds sang except for the best."

—Henry Van Dyke

Notice the derivation of a design from natural elements–in this case, grasses: (from right) hand-carved block of a stylized grass design, stamped onto paper, ceramic clay, and silver clay.

One way to derive designs from what you see in nature is to examine a small part of the larger whole. One fun approach to this is to take close-up images and then enlarge them even further on your computer or copier, filling the page. This process can render what was a detail into a main image, which may in turn be a design for other work. A shot of a tree, for instance, could instead be a close-up of tree bark. By enlarging an interesting section of the bark until it fills a page, it not only teaches us about the line and construction of tree bark, but shows us an interesting pattern of lights and darks, of striation and textures that can find their way into other works: designs for fabric, layers in a painting, or the surface of a ceramic tile. The rhythm of color that flows across the side of a mountain forest in autumn can teach us about moving from one color to another with gracious flow in a painting. A photo of a landscape can be analyzed for color and abstracted into watercolor washes, gradient layers of paper in a collage, or fabric choices for a quilt.

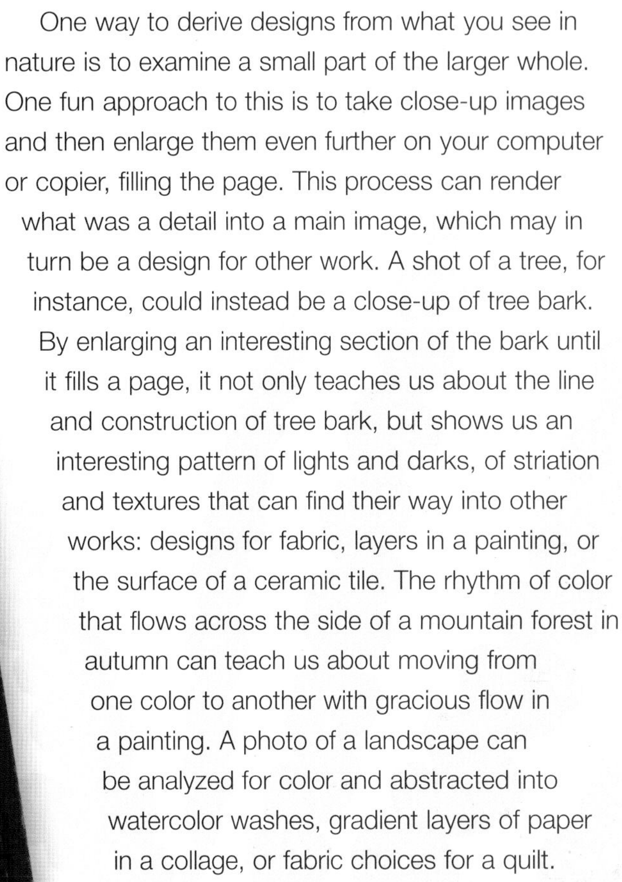

A separate journal can be dedicated to this sort of exploration. Often ideas need to be repeated, turned over, done in just slightly different ways until the right design appears. A separate journal can give a place to experiment freely without concern about designs that didn't quite work. In fact, when the journal is examined in hindsight—looking at the repetitious approaches, the repeated attempts at working with line and shape in various ways over and over—can provide an ongoing resource book for examining those shapes that intrigued us. Nature can teach us ways of delving into and more thoroughly exploring our art.

Mesh-printing, left; page 54;
Dye and salt printing, right; page 45.

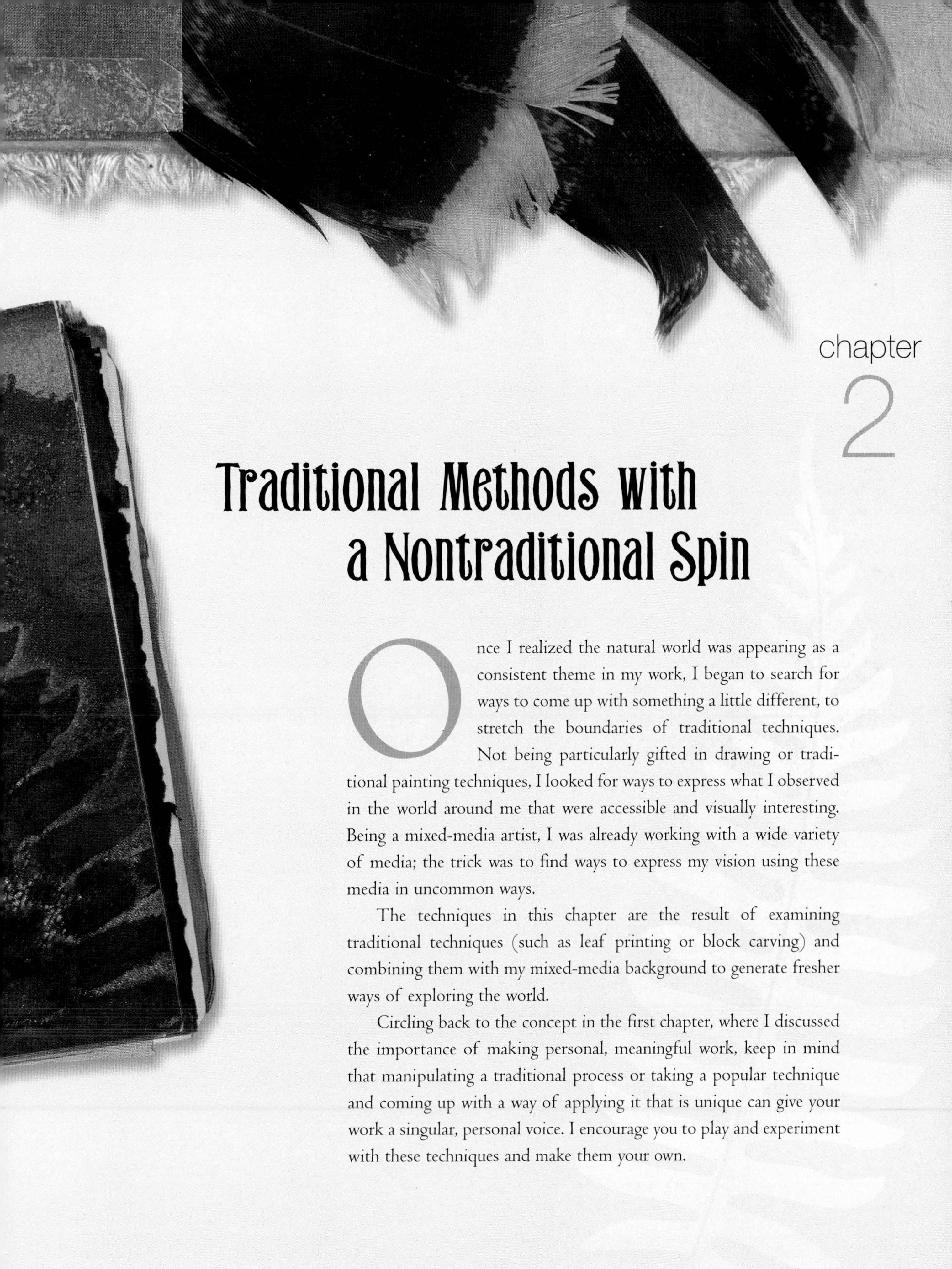

chapter 2

Traditional Methods with a Nontraditional Spin

Once I realized the natural world was appearing as a consistent theme in my work, I began to search for ways to come up with something a little different, to stretch the boundaries of traditional techniques. Not being particularly gifted in drawing or traditional painting techniques, I looked for ways to express what I observed in the world around me that were accessible and visually interesting. Being a mixed-media artist, I was already working with a wide variety of media; the trick was to find ways to express my vision using these media in uncommon ways.

The techniques in this chapter are the result of examining traditional techniques (such as leaf printing or block carving) and combining them with my mixed-media background to generate fresher ways of exploring the world.

Circling back to the concept in the first chapter, where I discussed the importance of making personal, meaningful work, keep in mind that manipulating a traditional process or taking a popular technique and coming up with a way of applying it that is unique can give your work a singular, personal voice. I encourage you to play and experiment with these techniques and make them your own.

Garving and Block Printing

Using images taken from nature to create hand-carved stamps, or printing blocks, has a number of advantages. A hand-carved block is an item that can be used repeatedly, and can move outside the pages of your nature journal. It can be pressed into polymer or ceramic clay, for instance, used in silver clay jewelry construction, or applied to paintings, other mixed-media pieces, or even simple cards. As each stroke of the carving tool reveals the block, the artist's hand is forever embedded in the image, making the blocks, regardless of their simplicity, personal artistic treasures.

Tip

Choose an image with easily definable areas of black and white. Too much detail can be difficult to reproduce with carving. Inverting the image, or printing it as a negative, will reverse the areas of black and white, producing additional carving options.

GETTING STARTED

Your image can be simple or complex. Carvings of simple lines sketched in graceful arcs can represent tall grasses or ocean waves. Circular strokes can depict stones in a riverbed or a beach of pebbles. A small block of irregular circles may be a perfect background stamp to depict snow or heavy rain.

A wealth of copyright-free imagery is available depicting things from nature. See a fox while hiking? Track down an image of a fox and he'll join you each time you use that block in your artwork. Keep an eye on the birdfeeder in your yard during a dreary winter, pull images of the birds you see, and turn them into a carved flock.

Photographs can be turned into carved imagery by using a black-and-white photocopier set darker than normal, or by manipulation in a software program such as Adobe Photoshop. One interesting use for leaf prints is to photocopy them, reduce the copies for carving, and carve the prints into blocks for future use.

Hand-carved blocks of flora and fauna, along with some stylized texture stamps of grasses and rocks.

"Never does nature say one thing and wisdom another."

—Juvenal

Once you've chosen your desired image, whether sketched or gathered from another source, photocopy the image using a toner copier. (Toner copiers are found at most commercial copy centers, but laser printers also use toner.) This gives you a chance to reduce or enlarge the image as needed. Also, multiple copies in multiple sizes may come in handy.

There are many different types of carving material. Mars Staedtler white plastic erasers, which come in two sizes and are available at office supply stores, are an inexpensive and easily obtainable choice, but because of their small size they limit the resulting image size. Linoleum block is battleship gray linoleum applied to a wooden block. It is very inexpensive but tougher to cut than an eraser, as it is very hard. Mars Staedtler also makes a product called MarsCarve, which is thick, soft, and easy to carve. It comes in a number of sizes. A number of companies produce alternatives to linoleum, including a brand called Speedy Kut. While much thinner than MarsCarve, it is also less expensive. Carving materials are available at art supply stores, some craft stores, and via Internet shopping.

The tools required to begin block carving can also be purchased at art supply shops, craft shops, and online. A block carving kit, or lino cutter kit, will come with a handle and several blades. The larger gouging blade is good for clearing large areas, while the small v-shaped blade is excellent for detail work. You may want to purchase an extra package of some of the blades or a second handle, which gives you two tools for carving without having to switch the blades in and out. A craft knife (such as an X-Acto knife) and fresh blades may also come in handy.

Materials

- image copied on a toner copier
- solvent: acetone, acetone-based nail polish remover, or a Chartpak colorless blender pen
- rubber gloves (if using acetone)
- cotton balls (if using nail polish or acetone)
- block of carving material
- black ink pad
- block carving tools

Carving medium with image transferred to its surface

INSTRUCTIONS

1. Trim the image from the toner copy to roughly match the size of the block (or smaller).
2. Place the image face down on the block and apply solvent to the back of the image in a circular motion. Carefully holding the image in place, lift a corner to see if the image has transferred sufficiently to the block. If it has, remove the paper and discard. If it hasn't, continue rubbing in a circular motion to transfer the image.
3. Once the image has transferred, remove the paper and discard. You are now ready to begin carving.
4. Clear the large blank area on the block with the larger gouge. To create detail strokes, leave carving material between the strokes in a pattern that highlights the main image.
5. Work close to and inside your main image with the finer blades.
6. Once the carving is complete, test the image by stamping it onto a black ink pad and printing the image onto paper. This will reveal any areas that need further refinement. Wipe the stamp clean before carving again.

Tips

Working on a Lazy Susan is handy for turning the work.

Place a dishcloth under the block to catch the discarded shavings and make clean up a snap: Just roll up the towel and unroll the discards into the trash.

INSTRUCTIONS FOR BLOCK PRINTING

The traditional way to print with a carved block is to squeeze printing ink onto a small sheet of glass, called a glass plate, and then use a brayer, or small roller, to apply the ink to the block. A sheet of paper is then laid onto to the block, and the backside of the paper is burnished with a baren or wooden spoon in order to make the image. In mixed-media work, however, applying the paper to the block isn't always a possibility. In many cases, it is necessary to apply the block to the paper or other printing surface.

The medium, or type of ink, used to print the block depends on the surface where the print is being applied. Options include printing ink, stamp pads designed for various surfaces, and even acrylic paint.

If you are using a small block and a stamp pad, press the block into the pad's surface. If the block is large, tap the surface of the pad against the block surface to cover it with sufficient ink for printing. When using ink and acrylic paint, use a cosmetic sponge to apply the pigment to the surface of the block.

Layered collage using hand-carved printing blocks of textures and a hand-carved printing block of a group of pine trees that had grown in the author's yard

VARIATIONS AND EXPERIMENTS

Printing blocks can also be used with other substances such as polymer clay, silver clay, or ceramic clay. Be sure to follow the necessary procedures for cleanly pressing an object into those surfaces. For example, rub the block lightly with olive oil before pressing into silver clay. The results of these experiments can be further incorporated into the mixed-media journal as a 3D attachment as shown below in this ceramic clay tile.

"Let us permit nature to have her way. She understands her business better than we do."

—Michel de Montaigne

A hand-carved printing block stamped into ceramic clay, and then after firing, colored with a wash of inks and mounted as an ornament for the cover of a journal

Monoprinting with Gelatin

Monotype, or one-of-a-kind printing using a gelatin plate, is a simple, nontoxic, and stress-free way of making soft, lovely nature prints. The method allows for a certain amount of playfulness and experimentation, as a variety of papers and pigments can be used in creating prints. You can work from colors in your favorite palette to echo feelings and experiences throughout your work, and the prints can be combined into work on other pages or serve as the basis for pages themselves.

Getting Started

In this technique, a printing plate is made from unflavored gelatin, and the gelatin plate is coated with pigment. Besides the fact that gelatin is inexpensive, a gelatin plate is sensitive enough to pick up a lot of textural detail from the objects.

The process of coating the plate is referred to as inking the plate. To make prints of natural materials, place them onto the coated plate, then press a sheet of paper onto the plate. A variety of natural materials can be used in this process, such as leaves, bark, flowers, and feathers. To make a negative print, place and leave the objects on the plate after inking; a positive print is made by removing the materials before the paper is placed on the inked plate.

Wallace Steven's poem, *Thirteen Ways of Looking at a Blackbird*, provided the inspiration for filling this Moleskin accordion-fold journal with positive and negative gelatin prints and stampings form hand-carved blocks.

"To find the universal elements enough; to find the air and the water exhilarating; to be refreshed by a morning walk or an evening saunter; to be thrilled by the stars at night; to be elated over a bird's nest or a wildflower in spring—these are some of the rewards of the simple life."

—John Borroughs

Tips

- Add a little sparkle to natural tones by adding a small sprinkle of gold or bronze Pearl Ex embossing powder onto the inked plate.
- Apply two or three colors to a plate the size of a cookie sheet for an interesting effect. Be careful not to create a mud color by blending too many hues.
- Use textile paint and print onto muslin or canvas.

Gelatin print using Lumiere acrylic paint

The instructions for gelatin prints often indicate the need for water-soluble printing ink or tube watercolors, but these products aren't a necessity. You can make the prints using inexpensive craft acrylic paints available at craft stores. These craft paints come in a wide range of colors, are non-toxic, and clean up easily. Fluid acrylics also work nicely and produce a matte finish. You can also use Lumiere paints (if you already have them on hand).

You can print your gelatin monotype on a variety of papers. Options include printmaking papers, rice paper, drawing paper, or even copier paper. If you use copier paper or inexpensive drawing paper, you will need to flatten your sheets with a heavy book after they are dry. Although white or cream paper works well, you can also print on black paper well with light-colored ink, which still registers quite a bit of detail.

Materials

- unflavored gelatin
- water
- cookie sheets with sides or jelly roll pans
- spoon or knife
- newsprint or scrap paper
- paper
- acrylic paints, water-soluble printing inks, or tube watercolors
- brayer
- small plastic tub or bucket of water (that brayer will fit in)
- natural materials for printing
- sponge
- paper towels

INSTRUCTIONS

1. Mix the unflavored gelatin according to the instructions for making gelatin blocks (also called squares or cubes), but use water instead of juice. Pour the gelatin onto the cookie sheet or jelly roll pan. (Depending on the dimensions of your pan, you may be able to fill two pans with one box of gelatin). If any air bubbles remain, pull them to the side of the pan with a spoon or knife. Let the pans sit while the gelatin sets up. Once set, refrigerate, uncovered. (Don't cover the pan or condensation will form.) The set gelatin forms a gelatin printing plate inside the pan. Avoid touching the surface of the plates. Refrigerated plates can last for several days in the refrigerator. Each plate is good for a number of prints, depending on the objects placed on them. If you are only using very flat objects such as leaves, you will probably get a dozen or more prints, as the plate isn't usually damaged or gouged by very flat objects. If your objects have more dimension, your plates will have a shorter printing life.

2. Arrange your work area so your materials are handy and you have a trash can nearby for discards. Spread newspaper on the floor or another flat area to create a place for the prints to dry. Prepare your papers by tearing them to the size of your pans (or smaller).

Tip

Make several plates and then store them more easily in the fridge by stacking them in a perpendicular fashion, crossing them over top of each other.

Zinnias make a surprisingly soft, floral gelatin print.

3. Squeeze a thin line of paint across the center of your gelatin plate. (You can apply one or more colors). Work the paint across the plate using the brayer to create a smooth, even coating. If you apply too much pigment, press scrap paper onto the plate to lift any excess. Place the brayer in the tub or bucket of water to prevent the paint from drying on it.

Tips

- If you made a negative print, you can print the image on another piece of paper, or place the sheet from your first print in the same place and create a layered print. You can also ink and add objects in between prints to add even more depth.
- If you made a positive print, keep a clean sheet of paper handy. Once you remove the object from the plate, "stamp" the object onto the paper to get another nature print. (See page 43.)

Feathers were stamped onto paper after the feathers had been used on a gelatin plate to create positive prints.

4. Place your natural items on top of the inked gelatin plate. Be aware that items that are three-dimensional will cut into your gelatin plate when the paper is pressed down. With your fingertips, gently smooth the items onto the plate. To make a positive image, lift the object back off the plate. For a negative image, leave the items in place.
5. Lay a piece of paper directly on the plate, and burnish gently with your fingers. Lift the paper off and place on the newspaper to dry.
6. If you left items on the plate in order to make a negative print, remove them.
7. Wipe the gelatin plate with a wet sponge. (The sponge shouldn't be sopping wet, but a dry sponge can dig into the plate; err on the wetter side to avoid damaging the plate). Sponge or lift off any excess water using sheets of scrap paper.
8. Repeat steps 3, 4, and 5 to create additional prints. When you are done printing, discard the gelatin into the trash can, not the sink, to avoid clogging the drain.

Tips

- One way to add more color is to ink an object, place it on the plate, ink the plate, and lift the object off.
- To cover small gouges in your plate and get a little more use out of it, cover the gouges with natural items and use those spots for creative negative nature prints. You can still use the other areas to create positive prints.
- To add text to your prints, let them dry completely and flatten them with a heavy book before feeding them through the printer.

"The poetry of the earth is never dead."

— John Keats

Dye and Salt Nature Printing

Cold water dyes are commonly used for fiber arts work. Several years ago, I began exploring the application of the rich, vivid color of these dyes onto my journal and artist book pages. The process is messy and accidental spills become relatively permanent. However, I haven't found anything else that stains the paper like ink while offering the vivid intense color of acrylic paint. Unlike paper painted with acrylics, the surface feel remains intact, and any three-dimensional texture from brush-strokes is eliminated. In addition, the paper can be smoothly folded without cracking, and there is no residual stickiness to cause the pages to adhere to one another, both characteristics that come in handy for certain book projects.

The selection of dyes in reds, russets, and cranberries; in olive, forest, grass, and spring greens; and in sky and deep blues are perfect for traditional leaf printing. The resulting prints are rich, deep, and tapestry-like in feel, as the way the dye is applied and soaks into the paper leaves very little, if any, white space. As with wet watercolor paint, sprinkling on Kosher salt creates a star-burst effect wherever the grains of salt land.

Consider making the prints in large batches, outdoors, on sunny days and then keep a stack handy in your studio. Note: due to the fluidity and permanence of the dye, this technique isn't conducive to working directly in a book. Instead, make the prints on sheets of paper, then add them to your journals.

Printmaking paper works very well with this technique, but hot press water color paper and some drawing papers will also produce good results. Using both full size sheets and smaller papers provides an interesting variety; work some sheets as background pages and some as vignettes or scenes.

Getting Started

You'll need a flat work area, such as a table top or floor. If you are working indoors, cover the floor with plastic sheeting first, then newspaper, to absorb the dye that will run off. Remember, the dye is permanent and does not come off other surfaces readily.

Materials

- several pairs of latex gloves
- cold water fabric dyes (Procion, DX)
- 8 oz (30 ml) jars with lids (one for each dye color)
- water
- shoebox or other low box
- printmaking paper (Rives, Stonehenge)
- 2" (5.1 cm) -wide inexpensive flat paint brushes (one for each color dye)
- flat, natural materials (leaves, grasses, ferns, flowers, feathers)
- small pebbles
- Kosher salt

INSTRUCTIONS

1. Wearing latex gloves, mix approximately 1/8 teaspoon (0.6 ml) of dye in an 8 oz (30 ml) jar of water. Repeat for all the colors you plan to use. Place all the jars in a low box, such as a shoebox, to prevent spillage.

2. Place your selected paper flat. Using a paint-brush, liberally coat the paper using one color of dye. Press your natural material flat onto the paper surface. Using the same color dye, cover the natural material. (It's okay if the dye seeps under the natural material.)

3. At this stage, there are several choices: Sprinkle the paper lightly with the Kosher salt or wait until you add the next or last color. Important: do not remove or disturb the natural materials. Resist the temptation to lift the natural materials to check on them. Let the papers dry completely.

4. Once the papers are dry or nearly so, apply a second color in sections on your paper, particularly around the natural material. Try tapping, dripping, or splattering. Work gently, and try not to disturb the material, as the leaves, grasses, ferns, or flowers will only be slightly adhered to the paper from the first coat of dye.

5. Sprinkle the wet paper with the Kosher salt, if desired, then let the paper and the dye under the natural materials dry completely.

6. Repeat steps 4 and 5 if desired, but use restraint: too many color additions may produce an unattractive, mudlike color.

7. Lift off the natural materials and discard.

▼ One color dye and salt print of oak leaf

Tips

This project offers a great opportunity to break out a color wheel and use complementary or analogous colors for great effects!

This technique will also work with inks, but it will be more expensive, and the color not as intense. It is also possible to use the same technique for very different results using watercolors.

▼ Two color dye and salt print of ferns; second color of dye applied while first color was still wet

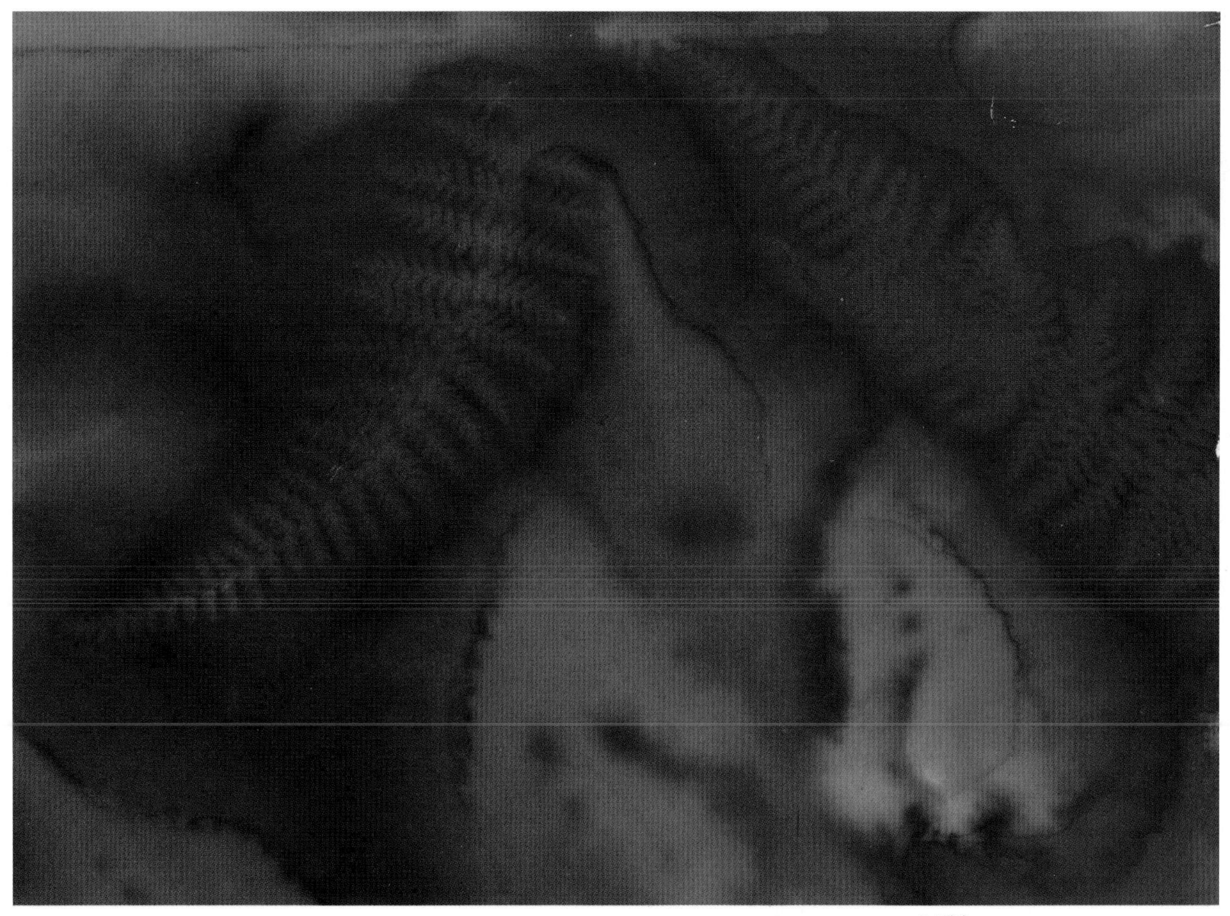

VARIATIONS AND EXPERIMENTS

1. Think beyond leaves, and print with feathers, cut fruit, weeds, grasses, and flowers.
2. Use watercolor crayons such as Caran d'Ache Neocolor II crayons to create multicolor prints. Start by choosing two or three crayon colors. Soften the tip of the crayon slightly with water. Color on the underside of the leaf or the surface of a feather and press onto watercolor paper.
3. Apply fluid acrylics to your natural materials using a cosmetic sponge, then place paint side down onto the paper, cover with clean newsprint or deli paper, and roll with a brayer.

▼ Features cobalt blue and spring green dyes. The blue dye and the salt were applied first. After these dried, the green dye was applied just around the oak leaf.

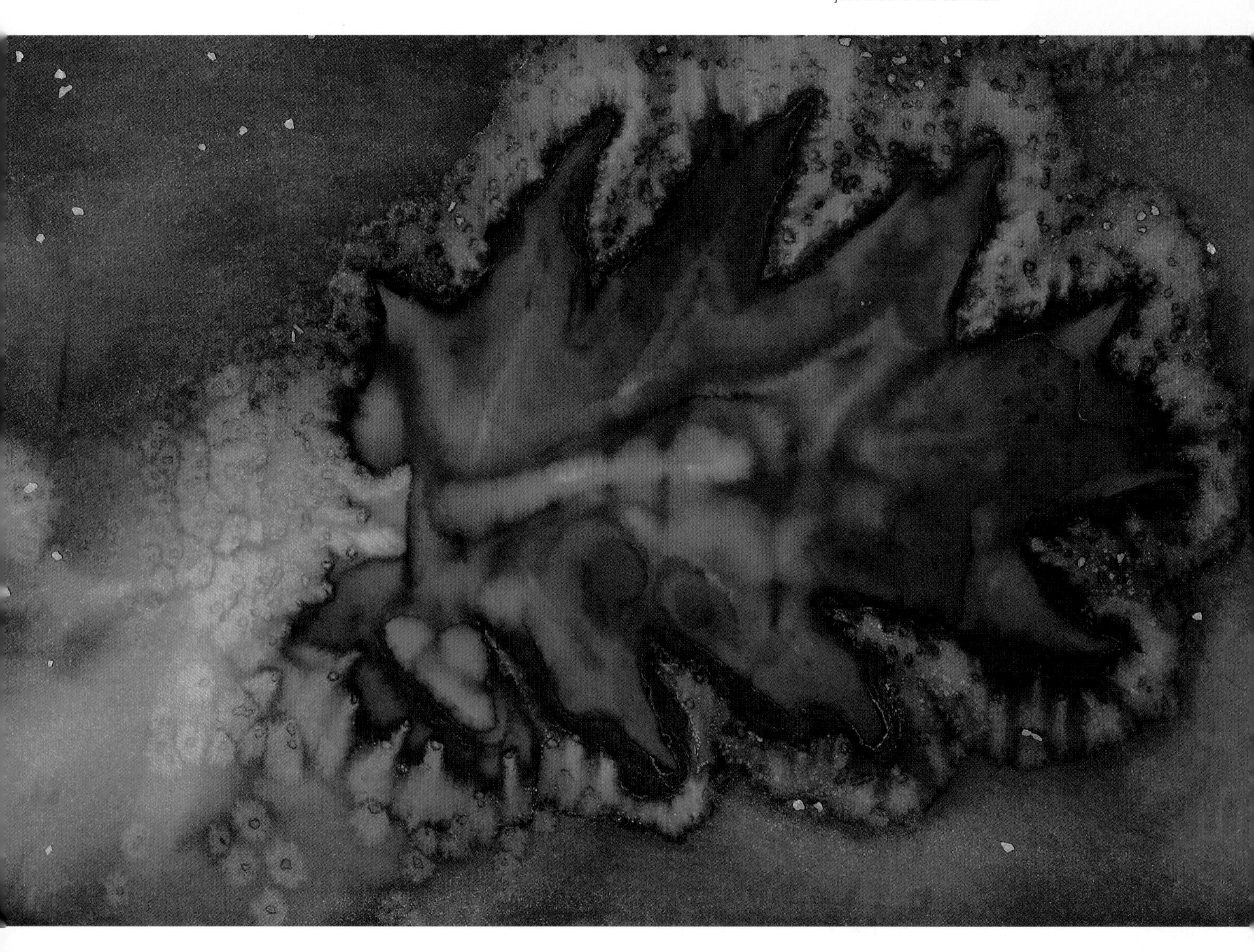

▲ Featuring a combination of two ferns, this print was created using two applications of the same color of dye. The first application dried completely before the second color was applied.

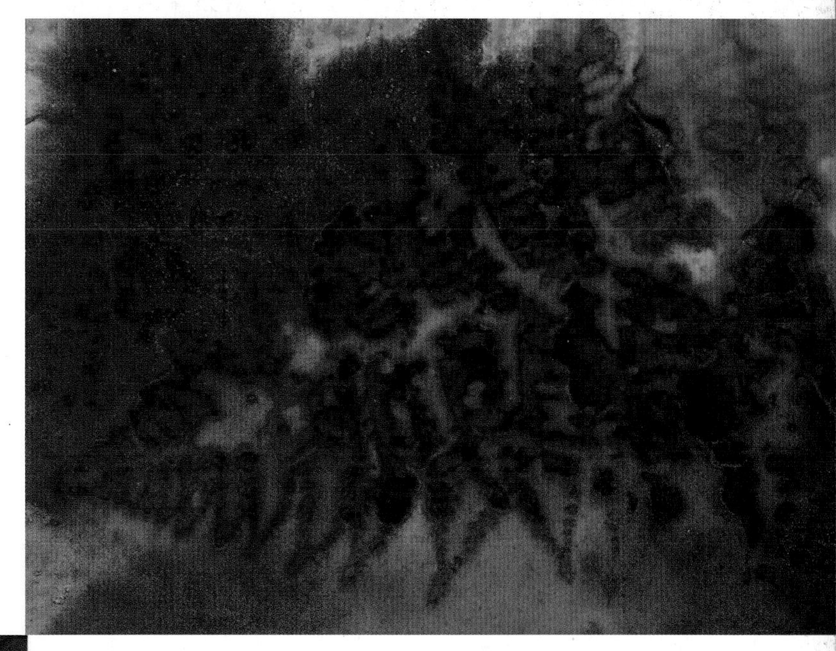

▶ This print uses ferns and features three applications of dye. The first was a garnet color, and while this color was wet, forest green was applied. After the first two colors had dried, the third color (rust) was applied around the ferns to create more emphasis.

◀ A combination of oak and maple leaves, this print also involves two applications of the same color. In this case, the second color was applied before the first color had finished drying.

Printing with Bleach

FIBER ARTISTS HAVE LONG APPRECIATED the effects of bleaching black fabric, also known as discharge dyeing. The contrast between the black and the bleached area is surprising, yet the edges of the bleached area are soft and organic. This technique is easily adapted to nature printing by using black paper as a substrate and common household bleach. As the black paper is bleached, a variety of colors can appear—gray, red, bronze, green, cream, or even gold, depending on the base of the black dye used in the particular paper.

To use this technique, dip or spray natural materials such as leaves, flat-faced flowers, or feathers with bleach, then press them onto the paper. Alternatively, materials can be positioned on the paper and bleach applied using a spray bottle to create a silhouette effect.

Bleach prints added as collage elements to a journal spread; two different papers have been used for slight color variations.

GETTING STARTED

It is important to remember safety when working with bleach; be sure to have adequate ventilation, preferably working outdoors. Just as when cleaning with bleach, replace the cap immediately after pouring the bleach, and never mix the bleach with anything besides water. Wear rubber gloves and old clothing.

You will also need to prepare a neutralizing solution. Because paper is porous, it will absorb the bleach; the bleach will seep through and continue to act on the paper, ruining your print. A neutralizing solution made of vinegar and water will stop the bleaching action.

Choosing the right paper for this technique may involve some experimentation. Canson Mi-Teintes black paper, which is commonly available in most craft stores, does not work. Arches Black does work, but is expensive. A large variety of other black papers will work, including black cardstock, text-woven papers, or the relatively inexpensive selection found in the scrapbooking section of craft stores.

I suggest keeping a record of what works and what doesn't. Also, test a small corner of your paper with a cotton swab dipped into bleach. Save a piece of each type of paper that works, and label it with the name of the paper and where you purchased it by either writing on the paper with a white marker, or by applying a piece of masking tape on which to write.

Materials

- plastic sheeting or painter's clothes for protection
- rubber gloves
- spray bottle
- household bleach
- water
- two buckets, trays, or small plastic tubs
- white vinegar
- masking tape
- natural materials, such as leaves, flowers, or feathers
- a selection of black papers
- scrap white paper
- paper towels

INSTRUCTIONS

1. Work in a well-ventilated area, and cover any surface that could be damaged by bleach, such carpets, drapes, or other furnishings. Wear rubber gloves while working with bleach, and keep your papers away from the bleaching solution or water.

2. Fill the spray bottle with a mixture of 1 part water to 1 part bleach.

3. Fill a bucket, tray, or plastic tub with a solution consisting of 1 part vinegar to 2 parts water.

4. Fill a second bucket, tray, or plastic tub with water. Label this with masking tape.

5. To stamp with bleach, spray the natural item and gently shake off the excess. Place the object onto a piece of black paper. Cover with a sheet of scrap white paper, and press your object down onto the paper. (The scrap paper prevents your gloved fingers from bleaching the paper.) Alternatively, to create a silhouette, lay the clean natural material onto the paper and spray the paper with the bleach solution.

6. The color will change fairly quickly. Moving quickly, remove the natural materials and place the paper into the vinegar/water neutralizing solution. After a few minutes, move your print into the tray of plain water. Dip it in and out a couple of times, then blot with the paper towels. (You may need to replenish both the neutralizing solution and the plain water trays after making several prints.)

7. Finished prints should be set aside to dry. You will want to rest them on a covered surface or, if outdoors, on the grass or concrete.

Tip

Once the bleached papers have dried, enhance the bleached areas with your choice of artistic media such as pastels, crayons, acrylics, or watercolors.

"Nothing is more beautiful than the loveliness of the woods before sunrise."

—George Washington Carver

VARIATIONS

Variations of bleach prints (from left, clockwise) Gerbera daisies; stamped grasses and ferns sprayed using a spray bottle

Nature Printing onto Metal Mesh

One afternoon, I was applying a couple of different patina solutions to brass and copper mesh and foil. I had placed sheets with solution on both sides on the grass to dry. It had been a little too long since the grass had been mown, and the grass pressed into the developing patina, creating fascinating patterns, textures, and even variations within the density of the patina color. I immediately began thinking about ways to control this process, and it occurred to me that I might be able to make traditional leaf prints using the patina solutions. Thus my experimentation began!

Here's what I discovered: Using commercially prepared patina solutions, you can create nature prints directly on fine metal mesh. The resulting sheets of mesh are intriguing and have a wonderful visual texture reminiscent of textiles. You can use them as individual book pages, as background to attach other nature journaling pieces, or as pockets to hold natural items. They can also be folded into frames for natural images.

Back inside cover of the *Tree Bark River Journal*, featuring a copper mesh pocket printed with locust leaves and a collection of wild turkey feathers inserted into a pocket; copper tape treated with patina solution forms pocket edges

Fern printed using Liver of Sulfur solution on copper

"Adopt the pace of nature: her secret is patience."

—Ralph Waldo Emerson

Materials

- fine-gauge metal mesh in brass or copper
- natural items for printing
- several pairs disposable latex gloves
- cardboard box
- spray adhesive
- rubber gloves
- safety glasses
- spray bottles
- patina solution (see the chart, page 56)
- clear matte or gloss spray paint
- garden hose or large bucket of clean water

Safety Tips

for Working with Metal Mesh

Metal mesh is metal, and any place it has been cut or torn will be quite sharp. Do not smooth metal mesh edges using your fingertips, even if you are wearing gloves. Instead, use a bone folder, wooden spoon, the edge of a plastic spatula, or a smoothing tool, or hammer the edges lightly with a wood or rubber mallet.

GETTING STARTED

Gather a selection of natural materials to use. Choose items that will rest relatively flat, such as tree or shrub leaves, ornamental grasses, ferns, flowers with flatter faces, thin sticks that have a straighter center line, flat rocks, feathers, slices of fruit—even grass clippings will work. Three-dimensional objects do not work well for this technique. Also, the object must block the mesh from the spray of patina solution, so avoid materials with obvious gaps or openings. I recommend having several choices of natural items available as you create the sheets of mesh.

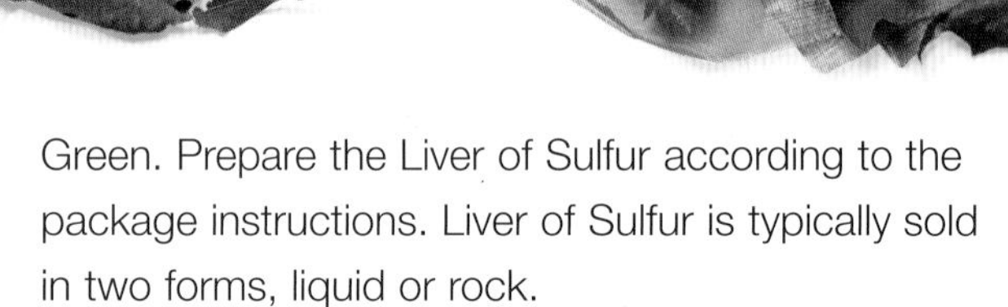

Prepare the sheets of fine metal mesh by tearing or cutting them into the desired size, then flattening to remove any creases or curl. The fine metal mesh will tear like fabric; simply snip where you wish to tear to get the process started. You can remove any creases and decrease the raggedness of the edges by smoothing the mesh with the side of a plastic spatula or a wooden spoon. A lightweight plastic mallet will also suffice.

This technique should be done on an unpainted flat surface, in an area with good ventilation, and a ready water supply. Working on a driveway, for instance, or a sidewalk with access to the garden hose is an excellent idea. If there is snow on the ground, work on a concrete basement floor and use a laundry tub. You will need to rinse the surface after this process, as the patina solution will dry, but still be present.

USING AND SELECTING PATINA SOLUTIONS

Patina solutions come in a several forms. You should proceed based on the type of patina solution you are using, whether Liver of Sulfur, Novacan Black for Solder/Lead, or Modern Options Patina Green. Prepare the Liver of Sulfur according to the package instructions. Liver of Sulfur is typically sold in two forms, liquid or rock.

The rock form would be prepared according to the package instructions, which includes cooking. This process is best done out of doors on a hot plate. The liquid version of Liver of Sulfur is merely diluted according to the package instructions. The other patina solutions, Novacan Black for Solder/Lead or Modern Options Patina Green, can be poured directly into the spray bottle. Choose your patina solution based on the metal you are using and the results you wish to obtain (see chart, below).

Which patina solution will work on which metal to produce what color results?

	Liver of Sulfur*	Novacan Black For Solder/Lead	Modern Options Patina Green or Blue
Brass	Will not work on brass	Brown to charcoal shades with green-blue to black highlights	Green or blue shades
Copper	Copper brown to black	Brown to charcoal shades with green-blue to black highlights	Green or blue shades
Pewter	Will not work on pewter	Gray to black shades	Will not work on pewter
Silver	Copper brown to black	Gray to black shades	Will not work on silver

** Liver of Sulfur can be manipulated using baking soda to produce golden hues and ammonia to produce iridescent blue hues. Detailed instructions for this process can be found in metal-smithing books and on the Internet.*

Safety Tips

for Working with Patina Solutions

- Patina solutions will eat away painted surfaces; you will want to work outdoors or on your garage or basement floor. You should rinse whatever surface you use very thoroughly with clean water.
- As patina solutions are designed to oxidize metal, they contain acid. If you touch the patina solutions with your bare skin, rinse the affected area immediately with cold water.
- Never mix patina solutions.
- Always wear rubber gloves and wear protective eyewear when using patina solutions.

INSTRUCTIONS

1. Lay the sheets of mesh on a flat surface. Arrange the natural materials on the sheets in a way that is visually interesting. For background sheets, arrange objects such as flowers or leaves all around the mesh. Alternatively, create scenes and painterly arrangements to serve as a focal point in a page or piece. (See image below.)

2. Put on latex gloves. Lift the natural materials one item or object at a time, place them in a cardboard box, spray them with adhesive, then adhere firmly to the mesh. (I recommend using a cardboard box for spraying, even when working outdoors, as any grass that gets sprayed with adhesive will end up glued to your shoes.) Replace latex gloves as needed and discard sticky ones.

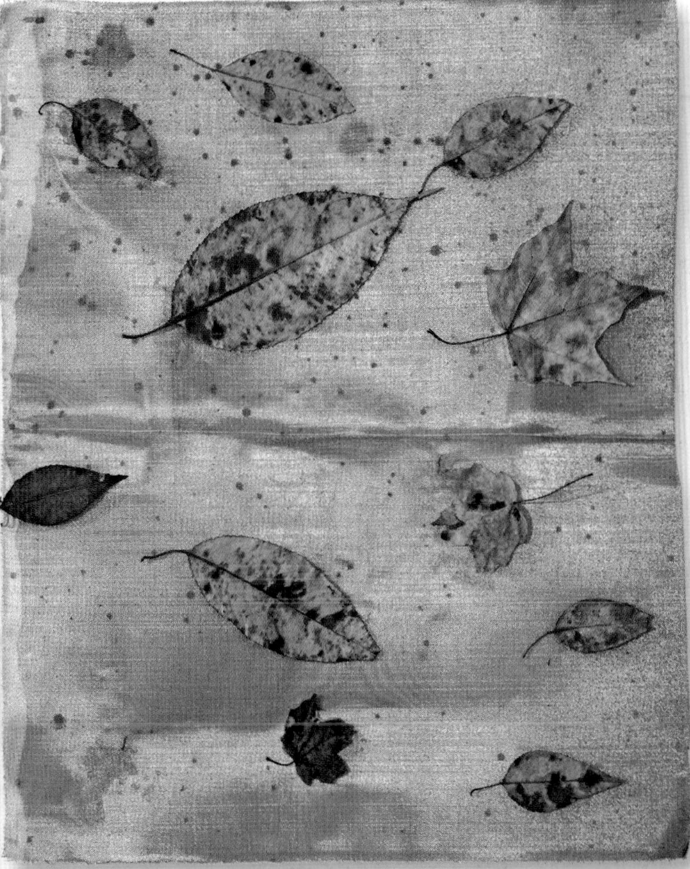

3. Once all natural materials are attached to the mesh, remove the latex gloves and put on the rubber gloves. Put on your safety glasses. Using the spray bottle of patina solution, apply one coat to the sheets of mesh. Allow the sheets to dry by clipping the mesh by a corner to a line or laying it out flat. The drying time varies greatly dependent upon the humidity level. Keep in mind that liver of sulfur continues to darken rather significantly as it dries, so use a light hand and apply the patina in layers. If working with Modern Options for patina solutions, apply the spray in layers to build up the blue-green rust that is characteristic of that product.

4. Once the mesh is dry, decide whether to apply more patina. If you are done, remove the natural materials, rinse the mesh, and let dry. If the mesh has large areas without patina, you can drip and/or drag patina solution through those areas using a leaf or a stick. Use this technique to create the illusion of veins on the leaves or simply add additional texture to the finished mesh. Again, rinse and let mesh dry completely. Be sure to discard the natural materials properly, as the patina solution on them is still a hazard.

5. Rinse the work area completely using a hose or bucket of water.

6. Once the mesh is completely dry, spray it with matte or gloss clear spray paint. Apply the clear spray to one side, allow the mesh to dry, then apply the clear spray to the other side and let the mesh dry completely.

VARIATIONS AND EXPERIMENTS

- Copper foil tape may be treated with an appropriate patina solution to give you an additional option for embellishment. Try using stencils, mesh produce bags, nylon netting, flat gears or washers, or stick-on letters from office supply stores to create different types of patterns and prints.
- Avoid items like paper doilies or lace because they will get soaked and transmit the patina solution to the metal mesh underneath.
- Natural items that have been pressed or dried are fragile and can be difficult to remove once they've been glued down. If this happens, simply scrape them off gently with a single-edge razor blade.

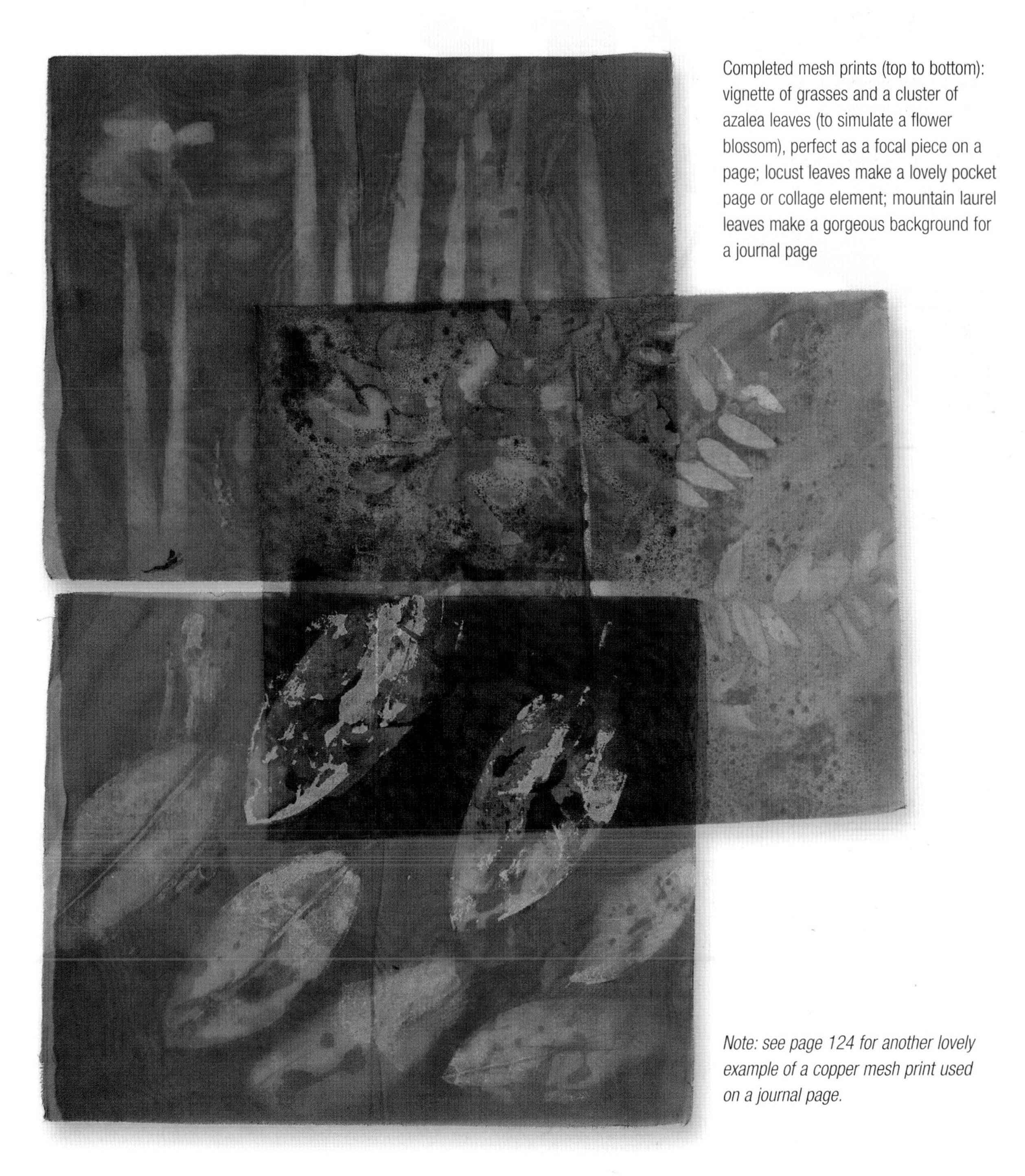

Completed mesh prints (top to bottom): vignette of grasses and a cluster of azalea leaves (to simulate a flower blossom), perfect as a focal piece on a page; locust leaves make a lovely pocket page or collage element; mountain laurel leaves make a gorgeous background for a journal page

Note: see page 124 for another lovely example of a copper mesh print used on a journal page.

Printing Natural Texture onto Metal Foil

You can apply a variety of interesting textures to copper, brass, or pewter foil using natural materials. The contrast can be starker than that created with metal mesh, but metal foil sheet can be printed to obtain a nice texture. One of the easiest textures to create is accomplished using grass.

Tip

Sometimes foil sheets come with a protective coating to prevent tarnishing. (Test a corner to be sure.) If you want your metal to tarnish, remove the protective coat by sanding lightly with 000 steel wool or a very fine sanding block.

Materials

- sheet of brass, copper, or pewter foil
- patina solution: Novacan Black or Liver of Sulfur based on chart (see page 56)
- spray bottle
- patch of slightly longer grass or a tray full of chopped ornamental grass
- source of water: hose, bucket, or utility sink
- clear gloss or matte spray paint

Grass texture printed on copper foil, accented with mesh printed with a feather

INSTRUCTIONS

1. On an unpainted outdoor surface, vigorously spray the metal sheet with patina solution.
2. Place sprayed side of foil sheet face down onto grass. Allow to dry completely.
3. If desired, repeat process to patina second side. Let metal dry completely.
4. Apply two coats of clear spray paint to each side. Allow each application to dry thoroughly before applying the next application.
5. Attach the metal foil to your work using eyelets, paper brads, strong glue, or double-sided carpet tape.

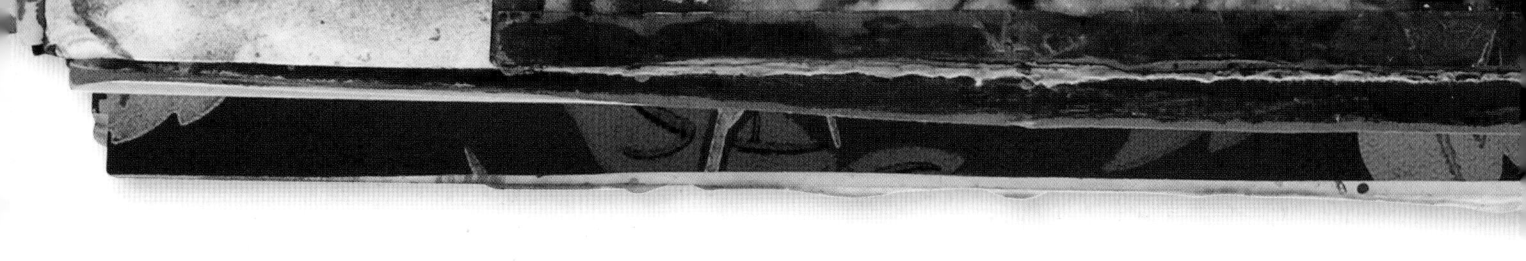

"Everybody needs beauty as well as bread, places to play in and pray in, where nature may heal and give strength to body and soul."

— John Muir

chapter

3

Image Creation and Generation

Creating a mixed-media nature journal with meaningful, intimate content requires imagery that feels personal to you. The content of the imagery in your journal takes the process up a notch, moving beyond creating a record of what you have seen to communicating your feelings around a subject. Whether you are working with original images or items borrowed from antique books, the way you manipulate those images can add to their meaning and make them uniquely yours.

One quick and easy way to capture your own, original images of nature is using a point-and-shoot camera. You don't need to be a professional photographer to generate wonderful, meaningful images of your very own. A digital camera makes the process even easier, as you can generate prints of your photos virtually on the spot.

Whether you are using vintage or original images, it's possible to change or enhance those items using a home computer and ink-jet printer. You can output prints on lovely or vintage paper, turn them into watercolorlike image transfers, make super enlargements, use decisive cropping, or employ intriguing transparencies. If you have a knack for working with image manipulation software, the possibilities expand a zillion-fold! Learning just one or two tricks with your photo imaging software can create many new possibilities. An ink-jet printer/scanner/copier combination is also incredibly useful for manipulating images.

Image Transfers Made Using Water

Image transfers offer fascinating artistic results. Any image or photograph you create can be placed on a copier or scanner bed and transferred to a variety of paper (and sometimes nonpaper) surfaces. Laser copies can be easily transferred with solvents, but frequent trips to a copy center can become inconvenient. A television documentary that showed artist Robert Rauschenberg working with transferring Giclée prints set a number of artists in the book-arts world experimenting with ink-jet ink, transparencies, photo paper, and water, me being no exception.

The method that follows is the one I teach to all of my classes, and requires only a printer, a spray bottle, and a wooden spoon. Without the toxic fumes of solvents, the process can be done on any flat surface, making it accessible to people with chemical sensitivities, or artists with children who work in home studios or on kitchen tables. Creating the copies and prints at home means there is no end to the creative manipulation of the image before it is transferred: You can reduce, enlarge, crop, change colors, add text, or layer with other imagery in design software, before the transfer even occurs. The resulting image has a soft, painterly quality, which is useful on its own or combined with other techniques.

Ink-jet transfers can also be made using gel medium. In this technique, images are printed onto photo paper or transparencies, gel medium is applied to the receptor paper, and the ink-jet image is applied face down and burnished firmly. However, gel medium is significantly more costly than water, and it doesn't offer many advantages to the water-based method.

Journal spread showing an ink-jet image transfer (leaves, center) and the remainder from the transfer (stones, left and leaves, right)

GETTING STARTED

Quite simply, this technique exploits the weakness in inexpensive paper, meaning the process makes use of the way lower-quality glossy photo paper will release a printed image if it becomes wet. Quality paper will not release the image as easily (which is why it costs more). You may be able to find a few brands of glossy ink-jet photo paper that work with this technique; in general, look for papers at the very bottom of the price range (they may be labeled glossy project paper) that feel slightly thicker in comparison to quality paper, and when wet, will become sticky. The right paper is crucial to the technique.

Materials

- inexpensive, glossy ink-jet photo paper (i.e. JetPrint Multiproject paper)
- computer
- ink-jet printer with regular, non-archival, non-pigment ink
- scissors
- spray bottle filled with water
- paper towels
- receptor surface: book page, printmaking or hot-press watercolor paper, muslin, or papers for experimenting
- wooden spoon or bone folder

INSTRUCTIONS

1. Select and print an image onto inexpensive glossy ink-jet photo paper. Trim any excess paper, leaving approximately ½" (1.3 cm) around the image. Set aside.

2. Using a spray bottle, dampen the receptor paper surface with water. Blot with paper towels and repeat the spraying and blotting process once more.

3. Using the finer spray setting, spray the paper very lightly. There should be no puddling, but instead a fine coating of water spray on the surface. Place the image face down on the receptor surface. Hold it in place with the fingertips of one hand, and use the other hand to rub the back of the image firmly with the bottom of a wooden spoon or a bone folder. Work across the entire surface of the back of the image.

4. Work quickly, because if the paper dries, the image transfer paper will adhere to your receptor surface.

Tips for Choosing Images

- This technique lends itself well to colorful images.
- Image transfers are less crisp and will soften details, so an overly detailed image with fine lines may not be a good choice.
- Create interesting effects by enlarging and/or cropping portions of images, for example, a section of a flower, a branch of a tree, or the eye of a deer.
- Don't expect a perfect reproduction. If your piece calls for a perfect copy, use a photocopy rather than an image transfer.
- Build layers over your transfer using pencils, pastels, paints, transparencies, text, sheer fabric, or tissue.

Check the work by lifting a corner of the image, while continuing to hold it in place. Once satisfied with the transfer, remove the ink-jet photo paper.

5. Set receptor surface aside to dry completely.

Image transfer on paper

TROUBLESHOOTING

If you get blotchy results, either the paper was not thoroughly spritzed with water, or you missed some areas during the rubbing process. If you spot the problem while peeking on the progress of a transfer, you can fix it by lightly respritzing the receptor paper surface, replacing the image, and continuing to rub these areas.

If bits of the photo paper adhered to the receptor surface, the receptor surface and the glossy photo paper dried together. You can sometimes fix tiny areas of this by spritzing with water and carefully removing the glossy photo paper. In the future, be sure to use sufficient water, or complete the technique more quickly.

Image transfer on fabric

If you get an extremely watery image, wavering lines, or ink oozing out from under the image, chances are you applied too much water. Use less water with your next transfer.

If you get no transfer whatsoever, several possibilities exist:

1. Your image is not printed on paper that will allow the transfer to occur.
2. You are using copies made on a laser printer or copier, such as those made at a copy center. These will not work for this technique, but may be transferred using a solvent called *xylene,* also found in graphic design blender pens. Information on this technique is described on page 68.
3. Your ink-jet printer is outfitted with archival or pigment ink. The less-expensive ink-jet ink is ideal for this project; quality ink is not.
4. Some ink-jet printers use only archival ink. Check your printer instructions.

Transfer samples: on fabric, top; on paper, left; on vintage paper, bottom

Image Transfers Made Using Solvent

If you have copies made at copying centers or offices on commercial grade copy machines, they are probably made with toner. The pigment is sealed to the paper with heat. In order to release this pigment to another surface, a solvent must be used. Laser printers also use a toner that is sealed to the paper with a heating element, and solvents are necessary to transfer images made with those machines as well.

When working with plain black-and-white copies, the two solvents you can use are acetone and xylene. Both of these chemicals are readily available at the hardware store and are shelved with other solvents and paint removers. Xylene is also found in a certain graphic design blender pen made by Chartpak, and you can also use this pen for transferring images.

Note: When working with color toner copies, you must use xylene, as acetone will not work on color copies. Also, solvents will not work with ink-jet copies (see Image Transfers with Water, page 64).

Solvent transfer using xylene in circle opening, center

INSTRUCTIONS FOR LIQUID SOLVENTS

1. Work outdoors, or in a well-ventilated area. Wear rubber gloves and a respirator, if possible.
2. Pour a small amount of solvent into a coffee can with a lid.
3. Place the image you want to copy face down on the paper to which you wish to transfer the image.
4. Dip a clean, white rag into the can and then replace the lid. Rub the wet rag onto the backside of the copy.
5. Burnish the backside with the bottom of a spoon. Peek occasionally to see how the transfer is progressing. Reapply solvent using the rag if needed until image transfer is completed. Set aside copy to dry completely and dispose of the copy remainder in an outdoor bin.

Materials

- rubber gloves
- respirator
- xylene or acetone
- coffee can with lid
- image to copy
- paper to receive copy
- clean, white rag
- spoon

INSTRUCTIONS FOR BLENDER PEN

1. Work in a well-ventilated space.
2. Place the image you want to copy face down on the paper to which you wish to transfer the image.
3. Uncap the marker and rub on the back. The fresher the marker the less pressure you will need. Peek occasionally to see how the transfer is progressing. Set aside copy to dry completely and dispose of the copy remainder in an outdoor bin.

Materials

- image to copy
- paper to receive copy
- Chartpak Colorless Blender pen

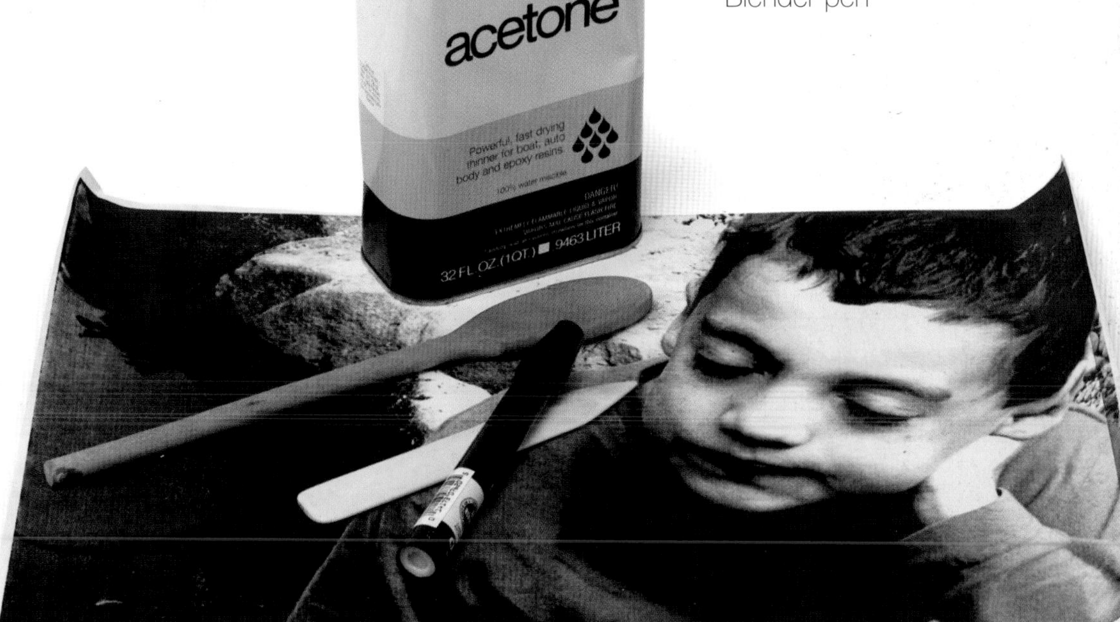

Working with Transparencies

PRINTING IMAGES ONTO TRANSPARENCIES OFFERS several possibilities for working with images:

- **Layering:** Transparencies can be layered over other images, or over each other to create images with depth. The transparency can be added as a separate page, with the subsequent page viewed through the transparency, or attached directly to the page.
- **Adding text:** Text can be added to a transparency by writing directly on the transparency with a permanent marker. Alternatively, you can add text by printing it onto a transparency and layering the transparency over the image.
- **Creating windows:** Cut an opening or window in a page and attach a transparency. Whether you attach the transparency from the front or the back depends on your preference and what your page needs compositionally.

because it has some
we like to think
cattail (kat'tāl) n. Perennial marsh plant,
Typha latifolia, with long flat leaves,
bearing brownish furry spikes.

CREATING A TRANSPARENT POCKET PAGE

You can use transparencies and metal mesh to create a pocket page for holding natural materials, other images, pages of text, or even small books.

Materials

- metal mesh
- bone folder or spoon
- scissors
- ruler
- eyelet setting tool
- 1/8" (0.6 mm) eyelets
- 1/8" (0.6 mm) hole punch
- hammer
- hard surface for pounding eyelet

Tip

Using mesh printed with the nature printing technique in chapter 2 for this project adds another dimension.

INSTRUCTIONS

1. Tear or cut the metal mesh into five strips. Two should measure at least 1¼" (3.1 cm) wide, and at least ½" (1.2 cm) longer than your transparency. Three strips should also be at least 1¼" (3.1 cm) wide and the same width of your transparency.
2. Fold the ends of your longer strips inwards ¼" (0.6 cm) on each end, setting the crease tightly using a bone folder or spoon. Do NOT use your fingers, as the mesh edges are very sharp.
3. Fold all the strips in half lengthwise and crease tightly.
4. Fit one of the shorter strips on the top edge of one of your transparency. Repeat for the top of the other transparency. Trim if necessary.
5. Fit the third shorter strip along the bottom of both transparencies.
6. Fit the two longer strips onto the left and right sides of both transparencies.
7. Using your ruler to measure, and your eyelet setting tool to create an indentation in the mesh sandwich, evenly mark a spot in each corner for the eyelets. Mark a spot in the centers of the bottom, both tops, and the left and right sides.
8. Punch holes where marked. You may need to disassemble the pieces to punch them individually.
9. Place and set your eyelets. The two pieces of mesh on the top should each have their own eyelet to form an open pocket. If you wish to eyelet your pocket closed, set all the other eyelets first, place your desired contents in your pocket, and then eyelet the top closed.
10. The eyelets on the side edge can be used to bind this pocket into a book or attach to another page.

"That we find a crystal or a poppy beautiful means that we are less alone, that we are more deeply inserted into existence than the course of single life would lead us to believe."

—John Berger

BIRD PORTRAITS IN COLOR
FEMALE

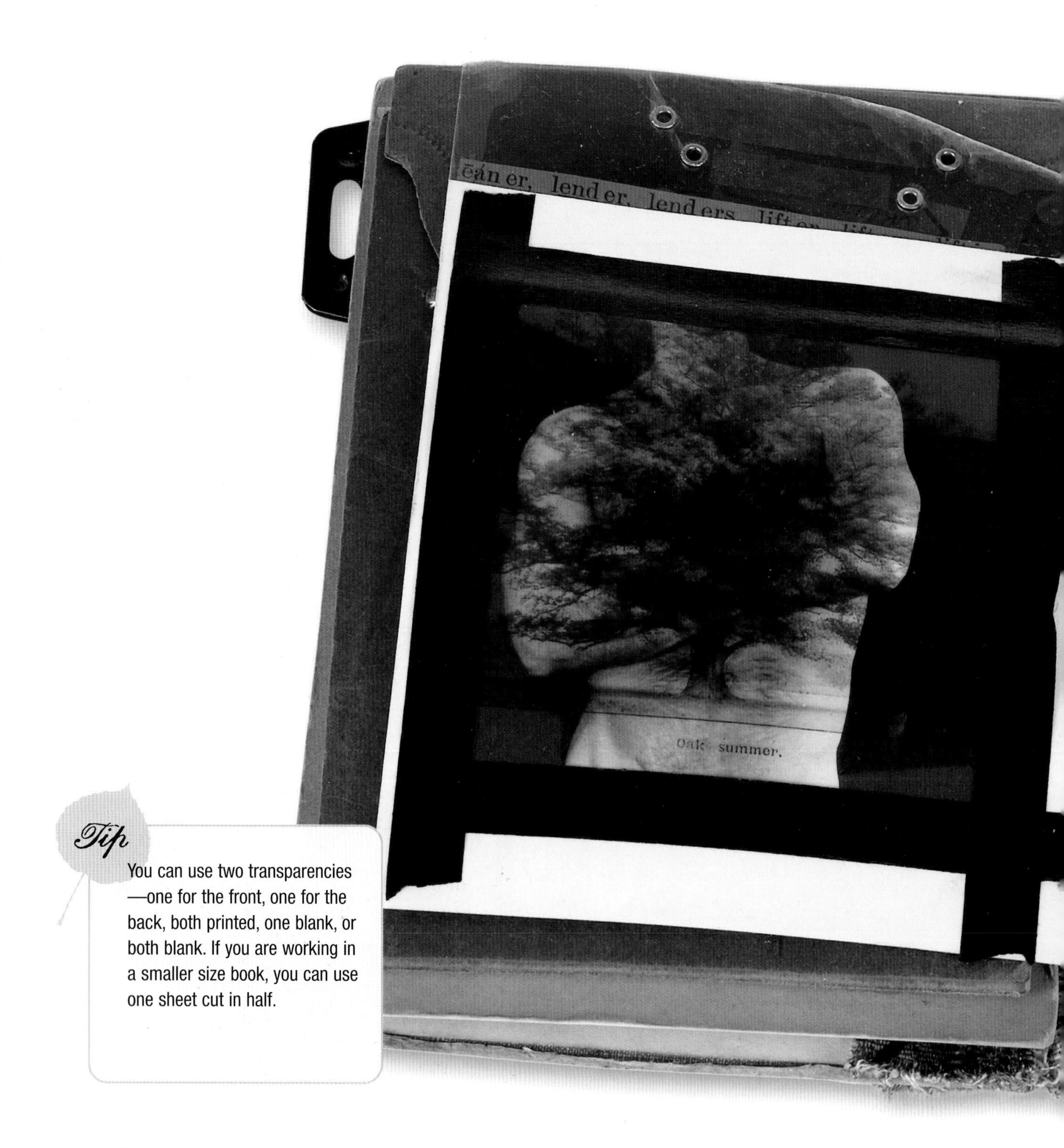

Tip

You can use two transparencies —one for the front, one for the back, both printed, one blank, or both blank. If you are working in a smaller size book, you can use one sheet cut in half.

"Look at the trees, look at the birds, look at the clouds, look at the stars and if you have eyes, you will be able to see that the whole existence is joyful."

—Osho

A
1
K
11
SUMMER RICH
Naked strength

Manipulation

Your personal collections of photographs and vintage materials can be altered to create fresh visual content. Even created images such as image transfers or photocopies can also be manipulated in ways that add even more to the visual message of that image.

Ink-jet transfers enhanced with charcoal and graphite (left); china marker and Caran D'Ache Neocolor II crayons (right)

PHOTOGRAPHS

An existing photograph printed on photo paper can be manipulated several ways beyond image transfers or photocopies. The actual photocopy can be sanded slightly, leaving behind reddish hues, or sanded a lot, right down to the base paper. The surface of the photograph can be scratched in areas or lightly cross-hatched with the end of a craft knife or an unfolded paperclip. This surface, in turn, can be embellished with watercolor crayons, permanent fine-point markers, oil paint sticks, oil pastels, colored pencils, china markers, and more. You can also use these media directly on a photograph without sanding. Be sure to seal the marked surface with a clear acrylic spray.

TRANSFERS

Transfers can also be manipulated. Mark-making can enhance the visual message of a piece; work into the image with pastels, colored pencils, charcoal, or markers. What's left behind from the transfer, the discarded piece of ink-jet photo paper, also makes a marvelous surface for crayons, pastels, and markers.

"Nature is man's teacher. She unfolds her treasures to his search, unseals his eye, illumes his mind, and purifies his heart; an influence breathes from all the sights and sounds of her existence."

—Alfred Billings Street

Ink-jet image transfer enhanced with colored pencil

VINTAGE MATERIALS

Vintage images can be copied or scanned and then printed on printmaking paper, ledger paper, or transparencies. Consider layering the image with text and then printing it on an interesting paper surface or a transparency. Vintage materials can also be transferred directly onto pages by copying them first onto ink-jet glossy photo paper and then using the technique described earlier in the chapter. They can be enlarged, reduced, lightened, or darkened on a photocopier. Vintage materials also make an intriguing surface for mark-making; practically any art media suitable for paper can be used in intriguing ways. Another interesting use for vintage papers is to use them as the base for leaf prints or for gelatin printing.

PHOTOCOPIES

Photocopies on paper are ideal for exploring mark-making, since copier paper is relatively inexpensive. Dry media pose no problems, so you can highlight, crosshatch, circle, and scribble with abandon. If you are using wet media such as watercolors, water-soluble pastels, or fluid acrylics, you will find taping the paper down with painter's tape onto a piece of scrap cardboard helpful to control the buckling of the paper. Mild buckling can be visually interesting on a page, but you may wish to flatten papers using heavy books before working them into your nature journal. You can use quality papers in a photocopier, and they will of course be sturdier for painting and mark-making purposes.

Photograph, professionally enlarged to 8" × 10" (20.3 × 25.4 cm), sanded, marked with a china marker, feathers, and sketches added

*"In all things of nature,
there is something of the marvelous."*

—Aristotle

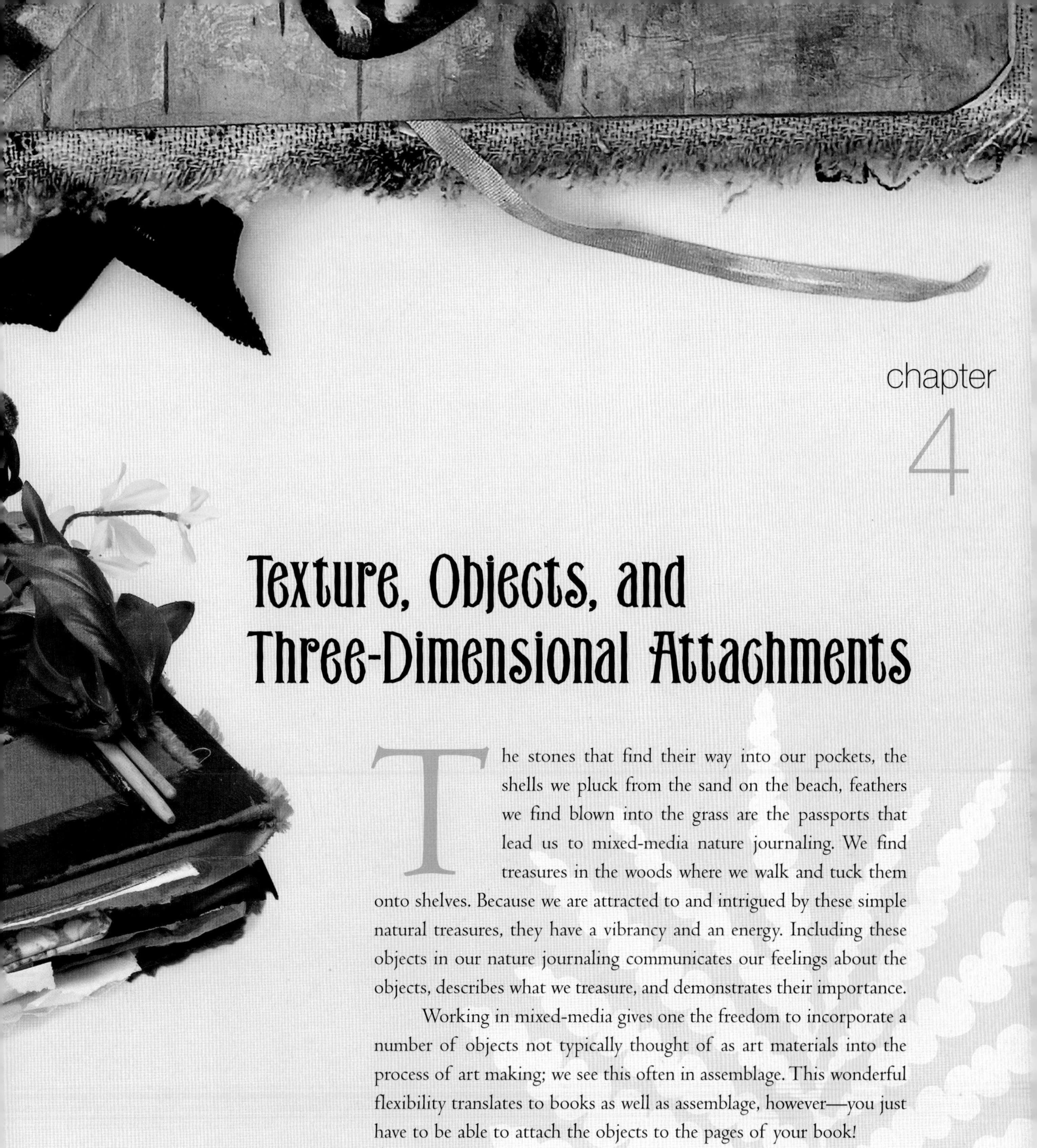

chapter

4

Texture, Objects, and Three-Dimensional Attachments

The stones that find their way into our pockets, the shells we pluck from the sand on the beach, feathers we find blown into the grass are the passports that lead us to mixed-media nature journaling. We find treasures in the woods where we walk and tuck them onto shelves. Because we are attracted to and intrigued by these simple natural treasures, they have a vibrancy and an energy. Including these objects in our nature journaling communicates our feelings about the objects, describes what we treasure, and demonstrates their importance.

Working in mixed-media gives one the freedom to incorporate a number of objects not typically thought of as art materials into the process of art making; we see this often in assemblage. This wonderful flexibility translates to books as well as assemblage, however—you just have to be able to attach the objects to the pages of your book!

Sticks and Stones... and Glass and Flowers and Leaves

The ability to incorporate found natural objects makes mixed-media interesting. Many of us are hunters and fishers of nature's discards and gifts: tumbled-smooth stones, lost feathers, a shed antler. We view these finds as treasures, and if we use them in our journals, it must be in a way that is pleasing. There are a number of ways to attach found objects to your pages, including wire, string, screws, double-stick carpet tape, eyelets, and/or brads or a combination thereof.

The best way to choose a glue is to read its packaging; this should tell you what types of material its designed for, the drying time, hardness, and whether it dries clear or not. I keep several different types of glue on hand including wood glue; a two-part epoxy glue; a liquid nails type of glue; glues specifically designed for glass, stone, ceramic, metal, and leather; and all-purpose super strong glue. I have certain brands I prefer, and have arrived at those based on my own experimentation. One other note: sometimes you have to rough up the surface of an object before gluing so the adhesive has something to stick to. You can do this using very fine sandpaper or steel wool.

Wire

Waxed Linen Thread

Wire is incredibly useful for attaching objects, especially anything that needs to hang freely, such as charms or tags. Use wire-wrapping techniques straight from jewelry making and use them to attach objects securely to your pages or to other objects. I especially like floral wire, as it comes in a dull silver color, is inexpensive, and is available in various gauges to suit my needs.

Waxed linen thread, often used in bookbinding, is a wonderful string for attaching or hanging objects. This thread is strong and is available in a wide variety of colors and thicknesses. The wax on the linen thread helps to secure any knots you make. In a pinch, you can substitute waxed dental floss for waxed linen thread. You can usually find three colors of floss: white, green (mint-flavored) and red (cinnamon-flavored).

Eyelets can be used to reinforce the holes in pages so the openings don't tear out and objects can be hung securely. The holes are made with an awl, a hole punch, a hand drill, or a drill bit used in a Dremel tool.

You can also use **paper brads** to attach objects to paper or other objects; simply insert the brad through holes in thinner objects.

Double-stick carpet tape is great for adhering thin, flattened sheets of tree bark or even thin metal to pages.

A flower press lets you dry and preserve flowers, leaves, and other plant materials for later use. The resulting dried items are fragile, however, so they are best attached with acrylic medium or sandwiched between sheets of mica.

Paper Brads

Eyelets

Double-Stick Tape

Working with Mica

Mica is a naturally occurring mineral that is mined all over the world. Human use of mica dates back to prehistoric times, and ancient Egyptian, Greek, Roman, and Aztec civilizations used it in artistic applications, such as cave paintings, pyramids, and sculptures. Mica is sometimes found in a form called sheet mica, which is available at art stamp or scrapbooking stores and through online suppliers.

The layers of sheet mica can be peeled into thinner sheets, allowing for a variety of uses. The thickness of the sheet impacts the color; the thinnest sheets are nearly transparent (like glass or acetate), while the thicker pieces have a sepia or smoky tone, depending on the the color of the mica sheet. Mica can be easily cut with scissors or a paper cutter, and you can attach it to your work using eyelets, paper brads, double-stick tape, or glue designed for glass.

Accordion-fold journal with mica enclosed photographs, transparencies, and ink-jet transfers as pages

"I'll tell you how the sun rose
a ribbon at a time."

—Emily Dickinson

Tip

Peel apart and trim your mica over a piece of scrap paper, and save the mica 'glitter' for adding a rich sparkle to other applications.

- mica
- scissors
- paper cutter
- double-sided tape
- glue designed for glass
- eyelets and setting tools
- paper brads

VARIATION IDEAS FOR USING MICA

1. As an individual page in a book: Peel a piece of mica into two sheets. Sandwich transparencies, paper, text, leaves, photographs, feathers, etc. between the sheets. Use eyelets or paper brads to affix the sheets together. Alternatively, use a mica tile as a cover for a hand-bound book.

2. Use mica as the front to a shadowbox. Affix the mica using narrow double-stick tape.

3. To create a mica window: Cut an opening in your paper that is slightly smaller than the mica tile. You can apply the mica tile to only one side, or split it apart and apply to both sides of the window using any of the previously mentioned methods. Trim the mica tile as needed or leave the edges more amorphous for visual texture (not shown).

4. To affix thin three-dimensional objects such as leaves, feathers, or ferns to a page: Arrange the object(s) on the paper, and place the mica tile over top. Affix using eyelets or paper brads.

5. To integrate and/or highlight an image on a cover or page: Use the sepia or smoky tones of mica to visually integrate and soften a stark image, while the visual texture of the irregular mica edges allows an image to be highlighted. This is a useful technique when working with a combination of vintage and new images, as a mica overlay gives new images a more vintage feel by virtue of its color palette.

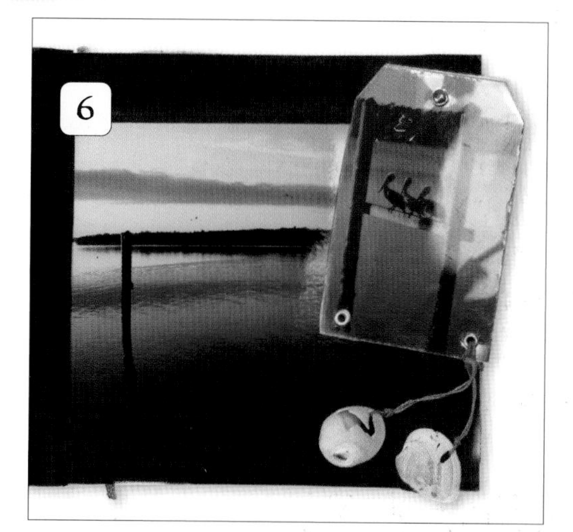

6. As a tag or charm to be attached to a page: Using a small piece of mica that has been split into two, sandwich the desired image or object in between and use eyelets to clamp the mica together. Tie the item to a page or cover using ribbon, fibers, thread, or wire.

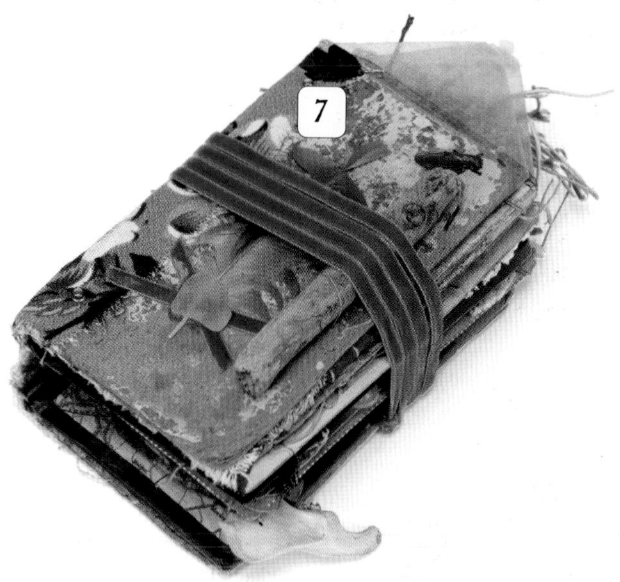

7. To extend the page beyond the traditional boundaries of the page or cover: You can create interesting edges and shapes using mica tiles. In this case, a house shape is created by extending mica tiles off the top of the page and throughout the book for thematic purposes.

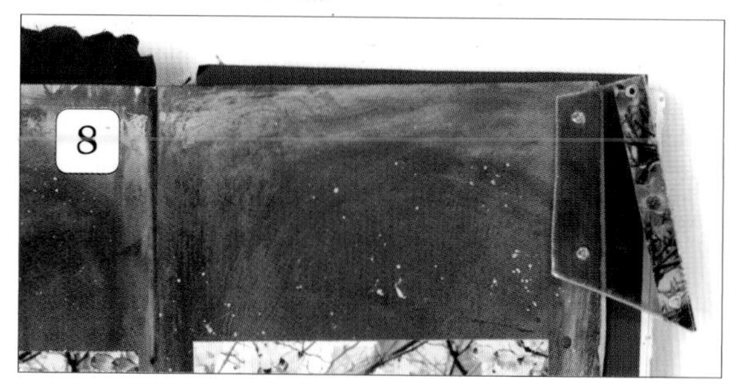

8. As an index tab: A small piece of mica can be split to form an index tab. Insert an image or text, then close the tab with eyelets and adhere in place using eyelets, brads, or double-sided tape. Alternatively, replace the plastic on an existing metal index tab with mica.

9. Combined with other materials to form framed tiles: Sandwich the image or a transparency in mica, frame the mica with metal mesh, and close it with eyelets. Conversely, you can also use mica as a free-standing frame or binding edge around a transparency or image (see pages 86–87).

Making Use of Artificial Materials

Artificial flowers and plants have come a long way in recent years. The realism of the materials makes them very useful for nature journaling. Unless I am casting them in resin or pressing them in a flower press, the forsythia near the river will not last long inserted in my journal, but quality artificial forsythia add a long-lasting yellow brightness to my journal pages. A wide variety of incredibly realistic floral stems and artificial ferns are available, from maidenhair to hart's tongue. Alternatively, use branches of oak leaves or individual leaves to add a pop of color to your journal pages when those leaves are busy returning to the earth beneath the snow.

Floral picks can add some unexpected interest via their glittery surfaces. Stems that simulate branches in silvery colors or in natural tones with little bells or buds in pearl or gold are a great way to convey a color palette and create feeling in your winter pages.

Flowers can be transformed into cover embellishments or removed from their stems and sewn onto pages and journal spines.

A variety of real sticks and branches are also available at craft stores, from bamboo, curly willow, and pussy willows to apple blossom branches. You can also find bird nests made of twigs and rushes, tiny birds or mushrooms made of Styrofoam, and both plastic or real blown eggs. If you want to add a taste of ocean life, objects such as shells, starfish, coral, stones, driftwood, and even sand are available at craft stores in case you don't live near a beach (or didn't pocket enough while you were there).

"How cunningly nature hides every wrinkle of her inconceivable antiquity under roses and violets and morning dew."

—Ralph Waldo Emerson

Wire mesh, with patina, folded into a pocket shape and attached to the page with eyelets

Working with Resin

Casting resin, and its close cousin, Envirotex Lite, are polymer compounds that produce a clear, thick, and solid coating. (Both products can be found in craft and hardware stores.) These products are very useful in mixed-media work, and mixed-media nature journaling is no exception. Using resin, you can incorporate objects that might otherwise have to be left out, including items that crumble (leaves or butterfly wings) or would get crushed (shells or flowers). You can also create arrangements of small, three-dimensional objects that might otherwise be difficult to attach individually with glue or wire.

The trick to using these products successfully is not really a trick; it is simply following the product directions for mixing the resin to the letter. These are two-part epoxy type products, so the ingredients must be measured exactly. Furthermore, vigorous stirring, if called for, must be truly vigorous—like whipping eggs with a fork or beating cake batter by hand. Be sure to stir for the entire length of time stated in the instructions. Failure to measure and stir properly can create resin that will not cure to a hard state.

Mixing cups are often available for sale where resin is sold. Dosing cups, such as those used to measure liquid over-the-counter medicines, are ideal for mixing small amounts. You can also make your own measure with a paper cup by determining how much it will hold, then marking the cup according to the amounts that will be mixed together.

Once you have poured the resin, don't be surprised if bubbles appear. To remove them, simply exhale onto the surface: The carbon dioxide in your breath will pop the bubbles. Alternatively, light a pencil torch or long-handled lighter and wave it above the surface to remove the bubbles. You do not want to touch the lit flame to the surface of the resin, as the resin will scorch and blacken.

Resin Shadowboxes

Creating a resin shadowbox is a visually pleasing way to display your natural materials while keeping them intact—shells, small bones, and other materials won't get crushed, and twigs won't dry out and snap. Also, because the resin dries clear, the objects will remain visible.

Getting Started

Start by deciding what to use as your shadowbox. Small wooden picture frames from dollar stores work very well, as do small, shallow breath mint tins. Remove the glass from the frames and seal the back closed; if the lid is attached to the tin, remove it using wire cutters. If necessary, spray paint the frame or tin using the color of your choice.

Materials

- shadowbox materials: papers, small shells, sticks, leaves, stones, bones, fibers, charms, beach glass, and/or tiny dolls
- decorative paper for background (optional)
- glue
- shadowbox: wooden picture frame; small, shallow cigar box; small, metal breath mint tin; or other container
- resin or Envirotex Lite
- mixing cup
- stirring stick (popsicle stick, skewer, chopstick)
- scissors
- freezer paper

INSTRUCTIONS

1. Gather the materials you wish to insert in your shadowbox. Consider using a decorative paper or nature print as the background and build the arrangement from there. Note: Thin papers such as a tissue or rice paper will not work; the resin will make the papers transparent.
2. Glue the background paper into place to prevent it from floating up from the background. Place the items in the shadowbox. Glue down any paper.
3. Mix resin or Envirotex Lite according to product directions. Bubbles may actually rise out of the compound while you are stirring; this is sign that you are stirring vigorously.
4. Place the shadowbox onto the freezer paper. This protects your work surface, and also lets you peel the shadowbox off once dry in case resin leaks under the box.
5. Pour the resin into the shadowbox until full. Exhale or run a lit torch over the surface to remove air bubbles.
6. Let dry according to the product instructions, typically 48 to 72 hours. Do not disturb until the product has set up.
7. Once dry, attach to book cover or page as desired.

"Nature does not hurry, yet everything is accomplished."

—Lao Tzu

RESIN-TREATED MIXED-MEDIA JOURNAL PAGE

Treating a journal page with resin lets you incorporate three-dimensional objects in a unique and protective way. Leaves, bark, bones, feathers, shells, and other fragile items can be laid on a page and incorporated into the design without worrying about them being destroyed.

You can also make a page to add to your journal by using a base of white tissue or deli wrapper papers. Applying Envirotex Lite renders the tissue paper invisible and the deli wrapper paper nearly so. These papers can then be layered over other papers and pages or serve as pages on their own.

Deli wrapper is available at warehouse-type stores such as Sam's Club or Costco. Deli paper can also be fed through an ink-jet printer, once trimmed to size, and will accept the ink without smudging. This is a nice technique for adding words to your resin-encased design. If you opt for tissue paper, it needn't be expensive, archival tissue; dollar store gift tissue will suffice.

Materials

- tissue or deli wrapper paper
- freezer paper
- background paper or fabric
- natural materials: small shells, sticks, leaves, stones, bones, fibers, charms, and/or beach glass
- appropriate collage materials: vintage imagery, photographs, transfers, magazine imagery, fabric bits, etc.
- liquid acrylic gel medium
- Envirotex Lite
- mixing cup
- stirring stick (popsicle stick, skewer, chopstick)
- spreading stick or discarded credit card (if making thin layer)
- sharp craft knife

Collage treated with resin; leaves on flowers were left unglued and lifted slightly using a toothpick to add dimension to page

BIRD PORTRAITS IN COLOR
Scale about one-half
MALE, WINTER
ROSE-BREASTED GROSBEAK
FULLY ADULT BREEDING MALE (BLACK WINGS)
FEMALE

INSTRUCTIONS

1. Lay deli or tissue paper on freezer paper.
2. Design the page. Adhere background paper and fabric with liquid acrylic gel medium. Three-dimensional objects should not be glued in place. To give paper pieces a three-dimensional quality, curve them outward, fold or lift them slightly in the resin (like leaves lifting off a branch).
3. Mix Envirotex Lite according to product directions. Apply the compound thickly, or use a stick or discarded credit card to create a thin layer. Thick layers allow for embedding objects more completely, while thin layers let you create a transparent paper that can be torn or cut. Exhale or run a lit torch over the surface to remove air bubbles.
4. Let the project dry according to the product instructions, typically 48 to 72 hours. Do not disturb until the product has set up. If you have difficulty removing the freezer paper, trim the edges with a sharp craft knife.

Thick, resin-treated page with bark, sticks, and leaves embedded in the resin

SUMMER

Incorporating Fibers

When you add fibers, you are adding color and texture. Ribbons, trims, yarns, strings, or torn strips of fabric can provide decorative embellishment to nature journal pages. Use them to add another layer, or as a new means of visually expressing what we see.

The sheer amount of novelty yarns available is astounding. Hand-dyed silk ribbons come in every shade imaginable and in multihued colors that seem custom dyed for nature journaling. My first trip into a yarn shop in years left me feeling as though I had walked into a fabulous candy shop. The array of colors and textures was overwhelming. I found myself wandering about picking up a balls of yarn in the colors of black basalt rock shot with white, the colors of the river as we run over it in a boat in the summer, the riot of color in my cutting garden, and the colors found on the beach and in shells from a recent trip to Florida. The yarn was soft, scratchy, firmly wound, loose and fluffy; some had tags of color bursting out everywhere. I left the shop with a large bag of these juicy colors and textures and without a good bit of cash!

Fibers work well on covers, on page edges, inside pockets, hanging off of eyelets, as book closures, or as embellishment to three-dimensional pieces. Fabric pieces can be worked right into a page just as you would use paper in a collage. I find gel medium or a good glue stick perfect for adhering fabric. Sewing fabric or paper onto a page is also an option. If you are working with fabric, running a zigzag stitch over yarns will effectively couch them to your fabric.

"The woods were made for the hunters of dreams,
The brooks for the fishers of song;
To the hunters who hunt for gunless game
The streams and the woods belong."

—Sam Walter Foss

House of Earth and Sky Journal

chapter 5

Pulling It All Together

Creating a mixed-media nature journal allows you to incorporate more of your own personal experience into your journals. Working with mixed-media gives you the flexibility to create on a wide variety of surfaces, such as paper, fabric, or found objects, and in a variety of structures such as sketchbooks, hand-bound books, altered books, boxes, or found objects. Working with three-dimensional objects inevitably leads to creative ways of housing your journaling efforts.

Mixed-media applications create depth in your work because of the layers you create with each successive technique or material. In this way, it can be used to accurately reflect the depth and complexity of your feelings. Any number of techniques can be combined on one or more surfaces to lend meaning and richness to your work.

"If the sight of blue skies fills you with joy, if a blade of grass springing up in the fields has the power to move you, if the simple things of nature have a message you understand, rejoice, for your soul is alive."

—Eleonora Duse

Structures and Housings

While it may seem like a narrow category at first glance, working in books and boxes offers virtually limitless possibilities for housing your work. Sketchbooks are available in a plethora of sizes and shapes, from pocket-sized to coffee table size and everything in between. They can be ring-bound, post-bound, feature sewn or glued spines, and be rectangular or square in their orientation.

Used books also offer a number of intriguing possibilities, and can be found in lots of shapes and sizes. You can work directly on the pages of these found books, although you may need to reinforce the pages by gluing several pages together. Having the text bleed through may be very desirable, or you can blank out the text with a wash of paint or gesso. Decorate the cover to your pleasing, or remove the covers and use them to bind a book of your own.

Vintage natural history books with intriguing covers and images

Choosing a vintage book on natural history often provides interesting cover boards as well as beautiful vintage paper and perhaps even images to use in your work. Look for vintage books covering specific types of flora or fauna (trees, ferns, birds, or animals), types of geographic locations (woods, beaches, or mountains), or specific locales (the Florida Everglades or the Grand Canyon). Online auction sites are a great way to find these gems.

Housing your work in a box lets you include loose found objects that might not otherwise work in a journal. A shed antler, a bird's nest, or a larger piece of driftwood can be tucked into a box, perhaps wired into place, and the remaining area filled with loose pages. Flea markets, auctions, craft shops, and cigar stores are great sources for interesting boxes or other containers.

The box below was originally designed to hold silver flatware. The surface of the box was sanded, then treated with Modern Options metal paint and patina solution. To further embellish the exterior, the artist attached a shed antler, an amethyst stone, and amethyst jewelry pieces using silver wire. The nest was found blown out of a nearby bush, and the bird was purchased at a flea market. On the inside, the bridge that held the flatware in place was removed to make room for pages and objects.

Alphabetical Nature Ledger

Seasons Journal

Tree Bark River Journal

Natural Design Journal

SETTING THE STAGE WITH A COVER

Covers are one of my favorite parts of making a nature journal. I typically begin a journal by making the cover. Whatever the theme or topic I am hoping to explore usually inspires the cover's embellishment. Someday, I am going to create a book consisting of pages made only of covers created around my favorite topics of nature exploration.

Covers permit us to make a statement about the direction we hope to go with our book. It may say something about color palette, the book's content, or it can set the atmosphere or mood of our journal. By creating the cover first, I am also free to evaluate it. If I don't like the cover, or I don't believe the cover works for a particular journal, I can set it aside for another project or discard it entirely, then start again without jeopardizing any journal content.

Covers can be very three-dimensional, extremely elaborate, or very simple in design. What goes on the cover communicates to the viewer what to expect from the content inside. Even if you are the only viewer, the cover sets the tone for that particular journal; this can help you creatively by giving you a jumping off point for the pages inside your book.

Surfaces

What will you create your work on? Paper? Fabric? Found objects? All three? In thinking about your nature journal, what surface you want to work on will, in part, shape what will house your work. Say you find a gorgeous piece of driftwood and feel inspired to embellish it with ribbons, fibers, wires, charms, beads, or paper bits related to your experience of finding the wood, visiting the beach, or walking in the sand with your son. The size and shape of the driftwood will determine what you will house that piece in, along with your other work for that journal process.

Paper is a readily available surface. Heavy, quality watercolor or printmaking papers will stand up to a variety of treatments without disintegrating and with only limited buckling. However, found papers, such as old ledger pages, maps of the area in which you hike, field identification guide pages, old 78 rpm record album sleeves, or Victorian photo album pages all make intriguing surfaces to work on. Papers are also available that incorporate plant materials; these can provide your work with another layer of emphasis on the natural world.

Fabric can offer an alternative direction for your work. Decorator fabrics with nature-related designs are everywhere; choices include ferns, vines, trees, animals, or even vignettes of natural scenery. Calicos printed with images of nature such as leaves, flowers, trees, and even stones are also easily obtainable. Muslin and canvas can also be used as a receptor surface for ink-jet transfers and gelatin prints.

You can also incorporate fabric pieces into paper collages, or turn a piece of fabric into an actual page by adding interfacing to provide stiffness. Interfacing is available at fabric stores in varying degrees of thickness, and comes in iron-on or stitchable versions. You can also print images directly onto fabric. A number of products are available at quilting shops and fabric stores for transferring images to fabric. Sheets of fabric, specially treated for use in a home ink-jet printer, are also available, as is a product called Bubble Jet Set (available online), which lets you treat your own fabric for use in an ink-jet printer.

A selection of fabrics and papers with natural elements

SINGLE SHEET BINDING TECHNIQUE

Working on a wide variety of flat surfaces and using three-dimensional objects doesn't mean you can't work in a book format; it merely calls for creative binding. To accommodate pages of various size and thickness and to create a book that will lie flat when closed, I recommend using a single sheet binding technique.

This easy technique requires very little in the way of materials but offers a great deal in terms of flexibility: each page is added to the book separately, meaning you can space the pages according to their thickness.

Tip

As you work your pages, be conscious of needing a 1/2" (1.2 cm) edge to place holes and/or eyelets for tying the binding. You can work close to the edge, but be conscious of the need for the holes so your pages aren't too thick.

Open spread shows pages sewn individually into spine

"The world is mud-luscious and puddle-wonderful."

—e.e. cummings

Materials

- piece of fabric
- scissors
- ruler
- Elmer's glue
- fabric glue
- cover boards (i.e. covers from an old book, davey board, or canvas board)
- ⅛" (0.3 cm) hole punch
- ⅛" (0.3 cm) eyelets
- eyelet setting tools
- tapestry or other large eyed needle
- waxed linen thread
- tissue paper for reinforcing fabric (optional)
- buttons or beads to embellish spine (optional)

INSTRUCTIONS

1. Cut the fabric to match the height of your cover boards and 8" (20.3 cm) wide. Glue the fabric onto the front cover board, overlapping onto the board at least 2" (5 cm). Set aside to dry. *[Figure 1]*

Figure 1

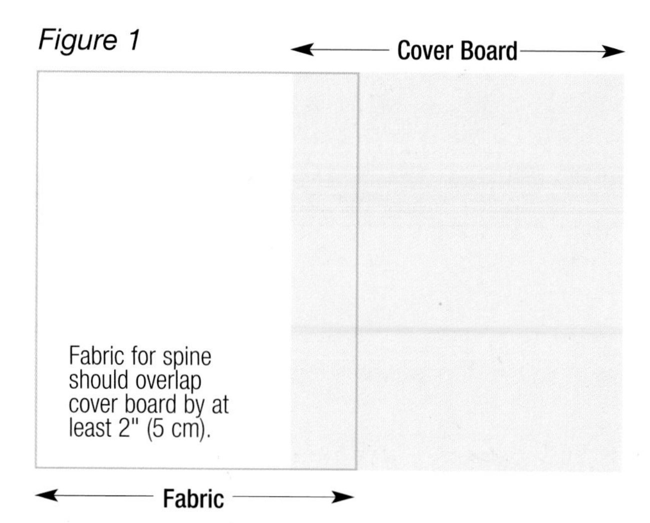

2. Create your pages. Embellish your journal cover, if desired.

3. On the left side of each page, approximately ½" (1.2 cm) from the edge, punch a ⅛" (0.3 cm) hole. Repeat. Two holes per page are sufficient, although you may want to make more. Reinforce the holes with an eyelet. *[Figure 2]*

Figure 2

4. Cut off a section of thread measuring at least 5" (12.7 cm) in length. Feed the thread through the hole and tie it in a square knot along the edge. Thread each end, one at a time, through the eye of a needle, and pull it through the fabric spine. Tie in a square knot. Add a bead or button, if desired. *[Figure 3]*

Figure 3

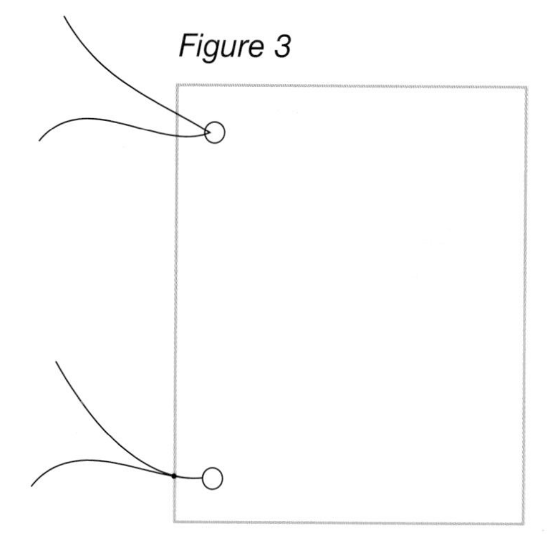

5. Repeat, as needed, to add additional pages.

Backgrounds

Spackle, a compound used to smooth cracks and fill holes in walls, can be used to create a textured background surface. This textured surface can then be treated with layers of colored glazes or washes of paint, or you can incorporate bits of natural materials or paper into the surface. You can further work the piece using graphite charcoal or other mark-making media.

Materials

- sturdy paper
- spackle
- putty knife
- sanding block, fine
- glazes, paints, inks
- clean rags or paper towels
- liquid acrylic medium
- mark-making media of your choice

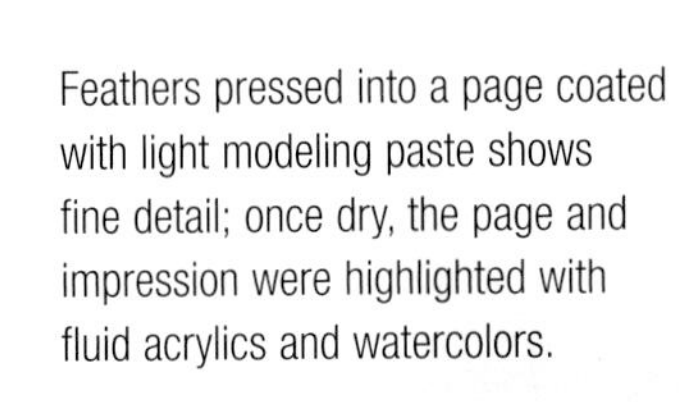

Feathers pressed into a page coated with light modeling paste shows fine detail; once dry, the page and impression were highlighted with fluid acrylics and watercolors.

"Nature is full of genius, full of the divinity; so that not a snowflake escapes his fashioning hand."

—Henry David Thoreau

INSTRUCTIONS

1. Apply spackle to paper using a putty knife, leaving peaks, valleys, and ridges (as shown, top left, opposite). The application should be thorough, but not too thick. Let dry thoroughly. If the spackle is still wet, the paper will be cool to the touch on the underside. Once dry, lightly sand down some of the texture if desired.

2. Glaze the spackle or apply a light-handed color wash (if the wash is too wet it will abrade the spackle; rag off some of the glaze by dabbing the surface with a rag or paper towel). Let dry. Add additional color before proceeding or add some collage pieces using liquid acrylic medium, and then add more color (as shown, above left). Let dry thoroughly between each application of wet media.

3. Continue building the collage by adding nature-related ephemera; texture; small, flat found objects; splashes of color; or drops of ink until the piece is finished (as shown, above). Let the piece dry completely.

PAINTING TECHNIQUES FOR BACKGROUNDS

The number of painting techniques for page backgrounds is astonishing. Here are a few ideas to get you started on exploring this as a way to start a page. Paper arts books and magazines often feature a wealth of these techniques, which are readily applicable to your mixed-media nature journals.

Layered collage using paint, tissue, ink, fabric, transparency and stampings form a hand-carved block

Materials

- two or three large stencil brushes
- two or three small stencil brushes
- disposable bristle brushes
- shallow dish or jar of water
- several colors of acrylic paint
- large pieces of cardboard or wax paper for disposable palettes
- baby wipes

SCRUBBED PAINT BACKGROUNDS

OPTION 1: Scrubbing it Off

In this technique, the paint is scrubbed off the page to create a wonderful surface reminiscent of granite or other stone, concrete, or fresco. This distressed look is similar to what can be done using solvent to remove paint, but in this case we are using baby wipes to remove the paint.

Working quickly, apply acrylic paint thickly, straight from the tube with a dry or nearly dry brush. Before the paint is dry, use the baby wipes to remove the paint from the paper surface with a scrubbing motion. Use additional baby wipes to lift even more paint from various areas until the look resembles stone. Blotting, compared to wiping the paint off in circular or straight motions, creates very different types of texture. Experiment to see what effect you like. If the results aren't quite right, you can always add more paint. If desired, let the paint dry completely, then add a second color and repeat the process. Various colors can be applied in different areas, and the textural effect can be different across the page.

OPTION 2: Scrubbing it On

Paint can also be scrubbed *onto* a page for textural effect. Using a large, stiff stencil brush (available at hardware stores), add paint to the page in successive layers. Stencil brushes will hold up to this sort of abuse more readily than acrylic art brushes, as stencil brushes are designed to be pounced repeatedly against a wall surface. This is a marvelous way of working in layers to create landscapes such as rolling hills, trees, rock faces, or atmospheric background color.

Inexpensive craft paints and fluid acrylics work well with this technique. If you are using tube acrylics, be sure to thin them with acrylic medium.

INSTRUCTIONS

1. Decide on a base color for your page, and squeeze some paint onto your palette. Pounce a large stencil brush into the paint, and move the brush to a clear area on the palette. Work the paint into the brush by scrubbing it in a circular motion. Take the brush over to the paper and using the same circular scrubbing motion, apply the paint to the paper. Rest the brush in a shallow dish of water between uses. Before using the brush on another color of paint, either rinse out the brush, or get it reasonably clean with a baby wipe.

2. If you are working on a simple background, repeat the first step to add additional colors using a clean stencil brush each time. (Darker colors will typically recede into a light background and vice versa.) This is a good technique for experimentation. If you act quickly, "mistakes" can be removed with a baby wipe. You may then have to go back in and rework your background color slightly.

To add extra texture to either the background or specific areas, use a disposable bristle brush, which applies paint with a rough texture.

If you are working on a landscape image, your next steps are determined by the landscape. In the sample on the opposite page, a simple landscape of trees was created by scrubbing a stencil brush in circular shapes to create the tree tops. Vintage paper was added to the center of each one. Highlights were added to the treetops by working in paint with a small stencil brush. The trunks were drawn in using paint and a child's disposable brush. Pencil and charcoal marks were made all over the surface. To form the clouds, the artist tore pieces of antique dictionary pages, then adhered them using acrylic medium. The clouds were highlighted using additional paint and a china marker. To make the dots, the artist dipped the wrong end of a paintbrush into a few complementary colors of paint, then stippled the wrong end of the brush on the surface.

"In some mysterious way, woods have never seemed to me to be static things. In physical terms, I move through them; yet in metaphysical ones, they seem to move through me."

—John Fowles

Back cover of
Seasons Journal

TISSUE PAPER LAYERING

Creating a collage on tissue paper or deli paper has a distinct advantage: the light weight of the base paper lets you easily attach the work to another surface, such as a book page or even a canvas. Using liquid acrylic medium to adhere the sewing pattern paper renders the sewing paper transparent over the tissue. Glossy liquid acrylic medium also lends the image a lovely sheen.

Materials

- freezer paper
- masking tape
- deli paper or tissue paper
- sewing pattern tissue paper
- liquid acrylic medium (gloss)
- nature-themed collage materials
- hand-carved blocks, textile stamps, or rubber stamps
- make-up sponges
- pencils, charcoal, or china marker
- large paintbrush
- acrylic paint (fluid acrylics, craft paints, lumiere paints)

INSTRUCTIONS

1. Cover your workspace with a sheet of freezer paper (the sheet of freezer paper should be larger than your deli paper or tissue paper sheet). Tape the corners of the freezer paper down with masking tape to keep it stationary.
2. Lay a piece of deli or tissue paper flat on the freezer paper. Apply a generous amount of liquid acrylic medium to the surface of the paper. Quickly lay a piece of sewing pattern tissue over the surface you just coated. Smooth with your fingers, then apply more liquid acrylic medium. As you do this, the sewing pattern tissue will become transparent. Begin adding collage items, such as the bird shown above right, onto the paper using the liquid acrylic medium.
3. Use hand carved blocks, textile stamps, or rubber stamps to add more visual interest. Apply acrylic paint to the stamp surface using a make-up sponge, as shown at right. Be sure to clean the stamps immediately following use. Let dry completely.
4. Using a china marker, colored pencil, graphite, charcoal, or other mark-making media, begin working your image. You can continue to layer sewing pattern or plain tissue over the collage, add more collage items, paint, or stamp as you like, as shown opposite.

"Just living is not enough. One must have sunshine, freedom, and a little flower."

—Hans Christian Andersen

BUILDING LAYERS

Mixed-media work is really about layers, creating meaning by combining techniques onto a page. Each new artistic technique you acquire is a new "word" in your visual vocabulary, a new way of expressing something—a feeling, an experience, a new way of communicating in a visual format. Layering techniques on a page is the visual equivalent of filling your journal pages with sentences and paragraphs. Just as words can be arranged in practically infinite combinations to form powerful prose, delicious mysteries, or moving poetry, the same can be said for combining artistic techniques. These visual paragraphs you create on your pages combine to tell a personally meaningful story by way of the entire journal.

Learning artistic techniques requires the willingness to experiment, to succeed and, yes, to fail. Don't hesitate to dispose of work with which you are not happy. Once of the biggest inhibitors of working in a journal is being afraid of "ruining a page." The page may not be what you had hoped, but the situation isn't permanent. Paint over it, remove it, cut it up, or throw it out. Start fresh—but just keep working.

Antique doll dress, filled with plant seeds and stitched to rice paper, inspiring Mary Oliver poem printed by ironing ribbon to freezer paper and running through the ink-jet printer

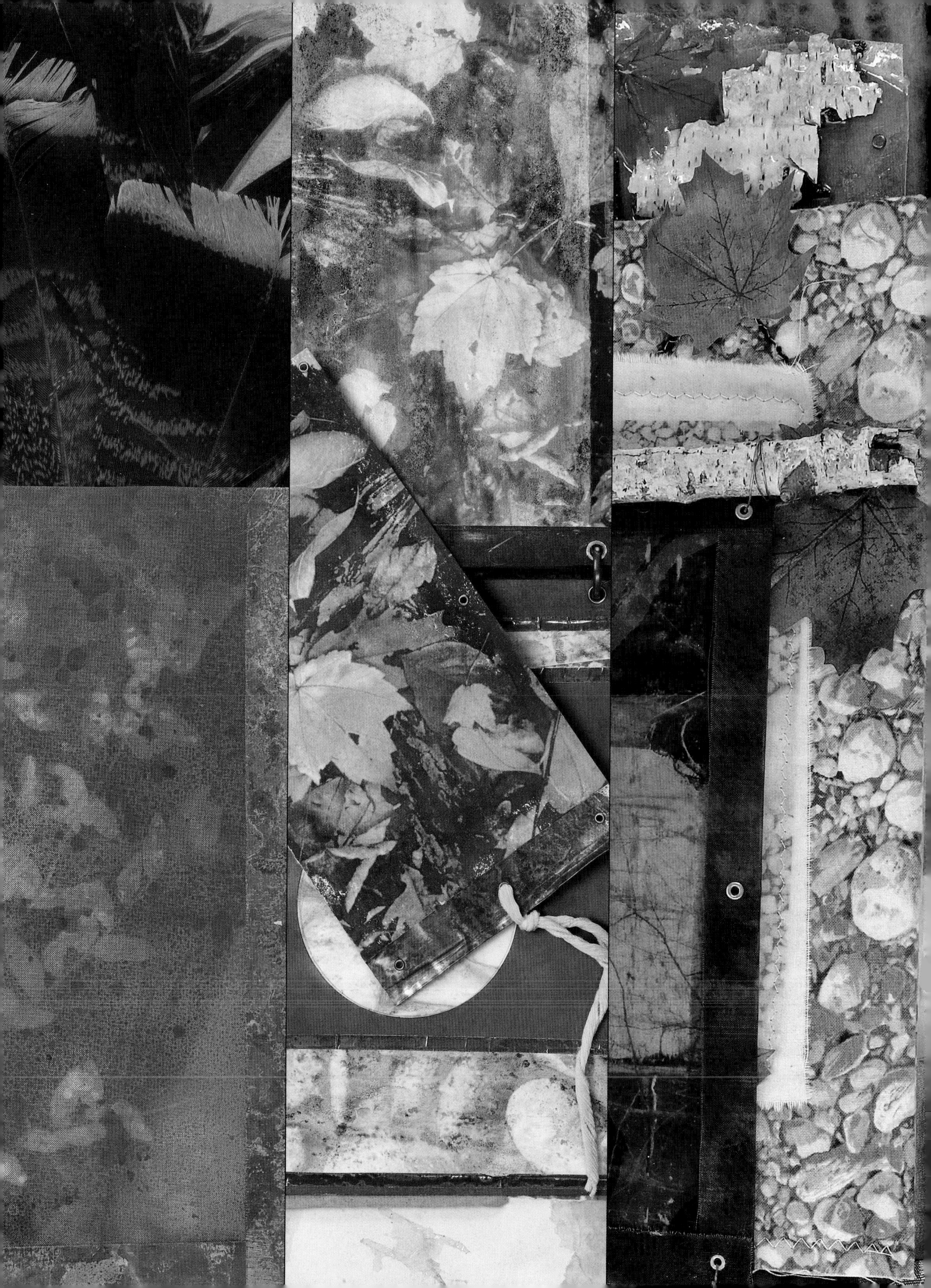

oak
fairy
king
Bright in spring
Living gold
ā corn, be fōre, be friend, be

Resources

www.amazon.com
JetPrint Multiproject Paper

www.coffebreakdesign.com
Mica tiles, eyelets, eyelet setting tools, paper brads

www.danielsmith.com
General art supplies, block carving and printing supplies, metal mesh, metal foil, Golden Fluid Acrylics, liquid acrylic medium, Brayers, Caran D'Ache Neocolor II crayons, printmaking and watercolor papers, sketchbooks

www.dharmatrading.com
Specialty fabric supplies, fabric dye, Bubble Jet Set

www.dickblick.com
General art supplies, block carving and printing supplies, metal mesh, metal foil, Golden Fluid Acrylics, liquid acrylic medium, Brayers, Caran D'Ache Neocolor II crayons, printmaking and watercolor papers, sketchbooks

www.jetprintphoto.com
JetPrint Multiproject Paper

Joann Fabrics and Crafts
www.joann.com
Eyelets, eyelet setting tools, paper brads

Lowe's Home Improvement Stores
www.lowes.com
Envirotex Lite

www.michaels.com
Envirotex Lite, Eyelets,
eyelet setting tools, paper brads

www.misterart.com
General art supplies, block carving and printing supplies, metal mesh, metal foil, Golden Fluid Acrylics, liquid acrylic medium, Brayers, Caran D'Ache Neocolor II crayons, printmaking and watercolor papers, sketchbooks, liver of sulfur

www.modernoptions.com
Patina solutions

www.ragandbonebindery.com
Journals and sketchbooks

www.usartquest.com
Mica tiles

Wal-Mart
www.walmart.com
JetPrint Multiproject Paper

About the Author

L.K. Ludwig is an artist living in Western Pennsylvania with her husband and three young children. After completing her undergraduate work in biology and graduate work in counseling, she decided to pursue her dreams by obtaining a degree in art.

L.K. teaches workshops nationally and in the occasional local college classroom. Her artwork and writing has appeared in the following magazines: *The Studio, Art & Life, Somerset Studio* (where she was profiled in the Artist Portfolio feature of the Nov/Dec 2003 issue), *Cloth Paper Scissors, Belle Armoire,* and *Shots.*

Her work also appears in several books, including *Making Journals By Hand; Altered Books, Collaborative Journals, and Other Adventures in Bookmaking; Artful Paper Dolls; Plush-O-Rama: Curious Creatures for Immature Adults; The Altered Object;* and *Mixed Media Collage: An Exploration of Contemporary Artists, Methods, and Materials.* Her work has also appeared in various galleries, exhibits, and venues across the country.

Copper mesh nature print with feathers using Liver of Sulfur, embellished with feathers, copper frames and other natural items

HEART OF THE FORES

Acknowledgments

As I worked on this book, I was expecting my youngest daughter; many people pointed out that writing a book was much like having a baby. Perhaps this is true, but the end result of writing a book doesn't wake you up in the middle of the night because it is hungry!

I'd like to very much thank Mary Ann Hall, my editor, for her gracious guidance and assistance, and Winnie Prentiss for this wonderful opportunity.

My parents told me many times growing up that I could do what ever I wanted if I put my mind to it, and it seems that I have taken that to heart in many ways. My mother, a painter, seems to have shared her creative gift. My father shared a deep, abiding love and respect for nature.

Glen Brunken, my academic advisor, mentor, and painting instructor, was the chair of the art department on the day I appeared at his door with the dream of finally pursuing my life as an artist. When I talked with him about entering the art program and the photographs I had been taking with just my eyes since I was a small child, there was no laughter, just complete understanding. His acceptance changed everything.

My soulmate and partner, Joe, who is an incredibly gifted artist, has offered steadfast support—including moving my entire studio during a summer heat wave while I could only watch and point. Joe, I love you more than day loves light and night loves sky.

And, no acknowledgments would be complete without mentioning my littles—Gryphon, Maggie, and Sunny Rose. You keep my eyes open wide and the wonder in the world around me fresh. I thank you for the magic and the tiny treasures thoughtfully brought home in pockets and clenched tight in small fists. Your mama loves you.